For years my friend Denver and I traveled across America hoping to make a difference. By the grace of God I met two young girls, Katherine and Isabelle, who are changing the world with their brilliant minds, pure hearts, and origami. I pray every student and parent will read this beautiful story and be inspired to make the world a better place for everyone.

Ron Hall,
author of #1 *New York Times* Bestseller,
Same Kind Of Different as Me

ONE PIECE OF PAPER AT A TIME

10 YEAR ANNIVERSARY EDITION

KATHERINE ADAMS ISABELLE ADAMS

RESULTS FASTER! PUBLISHING

Clovercroft Publishing

Some names of individuals have been changed in the book because of ongoing policy issues in their home countries.

For everyone who has supported us
unconditionally and believed that
two little girls can change the world.
But especially for Mom and Dad.

I will go before you and will level the mountains;
I will break down gates of bronze and
cut through bars of iron.
—Isaiah 45:2
New International Version

It has been said that something as small as
the flutter of a butterfly's wing can ultimately
cause a typhoon halfway around the world.
—Chaos Theory

CONTENTS

Foreword   xiii

Introduction: The Butterfly Effect in Real Life xv

2011 Crayon Economics   1

2012 Just *One* More Project   11

2013 Building Momentum   31

2014 And the Community Grows   57

2015 Our Work Expands   65

2016 Our Big Break   79

2017 Around the World   91

2018 Our Biggest Challenge Yet   139

Contents

2019 Conscious Leadership   187

2020 Covid Chrysalis   187

2021 A Grateful Heart   199

Epilogue   205

Acknowledgments   207

FOREWORD

I fell in love with Katherine and Isabelle a decade ago, long before their impact would be felt around the world. They joined me on stage at the Living Water annual event with such passion and poise when at five and eight years old, they began to inspire us all. They had a dream that they could make a difference in the lives of thirsty children, women, and men—by folding paper!

These co-CEOs, (and now their younger sister, Trinity, director of marketing in training), along with their incredible parents Deb and Ken are among the most impactful partners that Living Water is privileged to call friends. We are so proud to be their implementing partner in eighteen countries to bring Water, for Life, in Jesus' Name!

Their community, called Paper for Water, has enabled nearly $2 million in life-saving water around the world—245 amazing water projects in 18 countries—for people whose lives will be changed forever.

God blesses us with our unique experiences—our travel, our relationships, and our talents, like origami—and invites us to use our gifts to share His love! The girls have always used their gifts to invite others to make a dramatic, positive change in the lives of thousands of people.

I invite you to join Katherine and Isabelle on their journey as they embrace what they have been given to act, learn, and engage in an ever-growing, outward extension of love that has positively impacted the lives of 85,000 formerly thirsty people, hundreds of volunteers, and thousands of people who have been blessed by their story.

I remain poised at the edge of my seat to see what the Lord has planned for them and the impact that they will continue to make over the next decade. I am confident that you will enjoy these stories, and I'm excited for you as you create even more impactful stories and join with Paper for Water—to change the world!

Michael J Mantel, Ph.D.
President & CEO, Living Water International
Author, *Thirsting for Living Water*

INTRODUCTION
The Butterfly Effect in Real Life

According to Edward Lorenz, the mathematician and meteorologist most associated with Chaos Theory, a seemingly inconsequential influence like a butterfly flapping its wings can over time produce something as vast as a tornado. This is known as the Butterfly Effect. When reflecting on our ten-year journey with **Paper for Water**, our story has been shaped by God's hand and the ripple effects of our small daily actions that have produced significant and unforeseen results. To witness the Butterfly Effect in our lives, we have had to stick it out long term in a fast-paced culture telling us to constantly move on to the next best thing.

People rarely, if ever, talk about the Butterfly Effect in their personal lives because most don't stick around doing the same thing for long enough to notice it in the process. As a society, our attention span has become amazingly short. The advent of MTV was a game-changer, speeding everything up and increasing society's addiction to constant change and stimuli. 180 characters or less. Tik Tok videos. Disappearing Snapchat messages. And consider how Disney princess movies condition kids to wish upon a star to make things happen. This is not a recipe for success and longevity.

Organizations are teaching kids about entrepreneurship through lemonade stands, but one lemonade stand is just a taste. Kids may learn leadership through playing soccer, but one soccer season is just a warm-up. Some high schools require volunteer work to teach the joys of philanthropy, but four years of high school is just the beginning. Meaningful change takes time. It takes persistence, grit, and patience.

It's hard to believe it has been ten years since we set out to raise money for the first well in Ethiopia. During this time, we have seen the Butterfly Effect in real life because we've stuck with this project despite the temptations to move on to other things. We've persevered through long days and late nights, stressful moments, and seemingly unconquerable tasks.

This book celebrates the tenth anniversary of **Paper for Water** and gives a behind-the-scenes perspective into our journey. You'll see how one idea turned into a movement. Fold by fold, you'll witness how with the help of hundreds of volunteers and donors we have raised millions of dollars and transformed lives around the world.

Our small beginnings have grown and evolved to now impact 20 countries by providing hundreds of water and sanitation projects. We hope to not only show you how we got to this point but to spread our love of giving back by encouraging you to do the same. This collection of stories highlights the doors God has opened and our organization's butterfly effect in real life and the interconnectedness of the world. We hope our story and mission will inspire and resonate with your heart.

2011
CRAYON ECONOMICS

"One step at a time is all it takes you to get there."
Emily Dickinson

Isabelle

One person can change the world. For me and Katherine, there were two: our parents. The roots of the **Paper for Water** journey started with the people who laid the groundwork for our volunteering, crafting, and ingenuity. Our parents formed that foundation, one that we'd later blend into our own and channel into support for a cause that moved us, the global water crisis.

Growing up, Mom had always carried us to visit nursing homes in Dallas, and regularly, we volunteered at local food pantries or shelters too. These experiences of volunteering and helping others set the stage for all that followed. When connecting the dots now, one moment, one idea, one action always led to the next. Without the philanthropic base, we likely wouldn't have had our original dog and horse fundraising shows or started **Paper for Water**.

For as long as I can remember, crafting and DIY projects have been some of my favorite times with dad. They showed me how to make something with my hands and how to take an idea from a concept in the mind and bring it into the world. The experience taught patience and demonstrated one step leading to the next.

One day, he bought a jigsaw, and rather than make something boring and practical, he cut out a giant wooden dog and handed it to us along with some cans of paint. We were not exactly fine artists, but we had a lot of fun splatter-painting the dog and covering it with our little handprints. When we had finished covering it in layers of paint, he drew on a little face and a cute collar.

Katherine and I had so much fun that we begged him to cut out another… and another until we'd made at least a dozen dogs and had a little litter on our hands. My mother was not exactly pleased that our house was full of large wooden dogs, so my father, ever the entrepreneur, suggested selling our art.

Our dad was good friends with the manager of the local Starbucks, Andy Wisenhunt. So, one day, we went and asked if we could sell our dogs at his store. Given that we were only five and three, of course, he said yes. We then decided most of the profits would benefit Parkland's Pediatric Burn Camp, a charity our dad helped us choose.

Katherine and I traipsed through our neighborhood on a door-to-door advertising blitz to pass out flyers for our "dog show." Standing on tiptoes, I'd ring the doorbell and smile up at our neighbors while placing a handout for our event into their hands. The painted dogs raised around eight hundred dollars, which propelled us into the next venture.

With creative wheels turning, we crafted horses with more energy and flair. I raided a stamp collection (sorry, Mom!) and constructed bridles out of colorful, string tassels and added beaded trim.

Our first issue, and lesson, galloped in with the horse show. The detail was more ornate and appealing than the dogs, but our immediate circle had already purchased dogs. With a tapped market, we only raised $500 for Children's Medical Center. The event may have been less successful monetarily, but the entire experience was rewarding. And the idea to make a craft, sell the item, and donate the money originated.

Katherine

When school started in the fall of 2011, Dad would drop Isabelle off for school at Providence Christian School of Texas by 8 a.m., but my classes didn't start until 9 a.m.. After Dad dropped Isabelle off we'd go to Starbucks and I'd get a hot chocolate and Dad would get a venti iced coffee. Then we'd go to Westminster Presbyterian Church and Preschool where we were members. Dad was an elder and had a key, so we could hang out in the church workroom before my classes started. As you've already heard from Isabelle, Dad loves to make things. We'd make lots of stuff out of paper, like sculptures and drawings and at first, he taught me basic origami things like the crane and a box, but then he taught me how to make kusudama, Japanese modular folding. At first, it would take me about a week to fold 30 sheets of paper and assemble an ornament. But I thought it was fun. I made one for the church secretary and then my teacher and then the teacher's assistant and then the pastor and then the janitor and then they began to pile up around the house, which is when Dad suggested I have a show at Starbucks and sell these ornaments. When Isabelle heard I might be having a show without her, she got involved quickly and learned how to fold.

Isabelle

One evening in the fall of 2011, our neighbor Elizabeth Bowman, who had been on two well-drilling trips with Living Water International, heard that Katherine and I wanted to fundraise and stopped by, hoping to help us find our cause.

Elizabeth spread a photo album across the kitchen table and slowly flipped through the album. Page by page, child by child helping retrieve water. Barefoot families carrying water containers to murky streams that more resembled the color of hot chocolate than the clear water from our faucets.

The kids were my age and younger. Even at eight years old, I realized I had taken things for granted, like clean drinking water, and felt compelled to help. With the next turn, Elizabeth relayed world water facts.

> - *Millions of kids around the world don't have clean water to drink.*
> - *Many girls can't attend school because they have to fetch water.*
> - *Every 15 seconds, a child died due to a lack of clean water. (Now it's every 60 seconds).*

As I absorbed the information, I counted the seconds. *1, 2, 3, …, 15.* Katherine and I immediately knew that we had to do something to help. We couldn't decide which country we wanted to raise money for so we spun a globe and randomly stopped it. Our fingers landed on Ethiopia, and we set a goal to raise $500 towards a $9,200 deepwater well near Addis Ababa. With paper and a strong conviction, we set out to help change the world.

Given that it was September, we didn't have much time to make a Christmas ornament display at Starbucks happen. Luckily, our dad had already been in conversation with Andy at Starbucks, and he'd promised that we could have a fundraiser on November 3. We'd also be able to sell ornaments for the entire month of November.

Leading up to the event, Katherine, my dad, and I went to Starbucks to look at our ornament display space. The area Andy had selected for us was right where everyone stood around to wait for their drinks. Perfect, except for the fact that there wasn't a place to display our ornaments. A lot of people had hung framed artwork on the wall and there were hanging wires already in place for flat art, but there wasn't a good place to hang three-dimensional ornaments. I was stumped and worried, but I could see the wheels turning in my dad's head.

He pulled out a measuring tape and measured the distance from the floor to where we wanted to hang our display. Then, he measured the length of the wall and took a piece of paper out of his pocket, and sketched what a hanging ornament would look like there. Suddenly, I saw his vision and wasn't worried anymore. I'd seen my dad cut wooden creatures out of plywood, so I knew that this hanging frame would be a piece of cake.

That same weekend, after buying wood from Home Depot, we got to work. Dad cut out the pieces with his saw; Katherine and I glued them together, and after we'd sanded and applied the first coat of green and red paint, I thought, *This is going to look pretty cool.*

When we did our dog and horse fundraising shows, Dad had taught us how to use Microsoft Publisher. So together we designed a cute flyer advertising our first origami show. I invited all of my classmates, all of my teachers, all of our church friends, and nudged Mom and Dad to invite all of their acquaintances and neighbors.

Pretty soon, word traveled throughout our community. Some people who were regulars at Starbucks and knew my parents got wind of what we were doing and passed the information to Ken Lampton. Ken, a local real estate agent, used a few of his weekly advertising spots in the local newspaper and magazines to publicize our fundraiser next to his real estate listings. So when November 3 rolled around, at least 100 people showed up!

At the event, we hung a world map next to a wreath decorated with origami alongside our individual ornaments. Katherine did ten-minute folding demonstrations while I stood next to the ornaments and answered everyone's questions about what we were doing, how we were trying to raise money, why we were doing it, and where in the world Ethiopia was. Our sister Trinity entertained everyone with a wooden snake that our friend, "Uncle" Ron had brought for her. And of course, "Uncle" Ron was there to encourage us with our project.

So many members of our community rallied their support behind us. My first-grade teacher Mrs. Thornhill showed up and was one of the most supportive people there! At the last minute, my mom was concerned that people wouldn't be able to safely carry their ornaments home. So she had ordered awesome little checkered boxes. Mrs. Thornhill gushed about how professional we were in our presentation, right down to what people could use to give the ornaments to others. (Thanks, Mom!)

Elizabeth, who'd convinced us to choose water as our charity for the month, attended and bought four or five ornaments. Mr. Lampton, the real estate agent, brought his wife, who was principal of the local elementary school. She bought ten ornaments for her favorite teachers and promised to order 20 more. A number of the medical staff at my father's hospital showed up and all bought ornaments.

The time went by quickly, and at the end of the evening, we had been there for at least three hours. I'd probably told the story of our last two months of work 50 times and was pretty worn out. I perked up though because we were able to declare, "We sold out!"

Shocked on the car ride home, I said, "I can't believe we sold out of ornaments."

Dad asked, "Okay, girls, so what's the next step?"

Katherine and I looked at one another, and said, "We've got to make more ornaments!"

A little smirk slid across his face, "No, you need to raise your prices."

Once home, he instructed us to sit at the kitchen table while he dug through drawers to find paper and crayons. Sitting next to us, he drew a graph in blue and green crayons. He labeled the vertical axis the price of the ornaments, and the horizontal axis the number of ornaments people wanted.

"Okay, supply and demand," he said, "Look at the demand curve: when the line goes down, the price is going down and the demand for the item typically increases. But if you set your prices too high, fewer people will order ornaments. What we need to find is the equilibrium where the price meets the demand. When the item is scarce, like the ornaments, and the demand is high, the price needs to rise."

After that evening's After Action review and economics lessons, we raised prices, decided to make more ornaments, and shifted the goal to raise money for the entire well in Ethiopia.

Mom wasn't fully on board yet folding. So the folding crew consisted of Katherine, Dad, and me. When people began ordering ten or twelve at a time, we could barely fold fast enough. Every spare moment, we made ornaments... in the car, while doing homework, after church. We folded all day every day, barely meeting the demand. Mom quickly joined us and the load became easier. Before the end of the year, the *Dallas Morning News* and the *White Rock News* wrote an article about our mission and the orders increased even more.

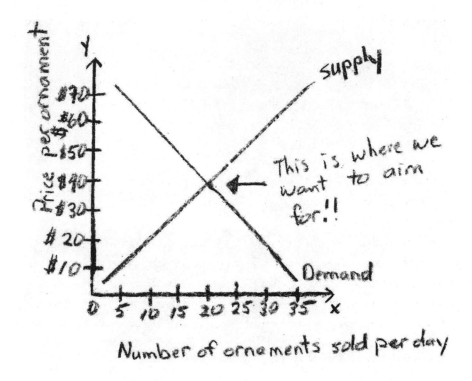

A friend introduced our dad to Curtis Eggmeyer, the CEO of LemiShine. You know the awesome earth-friendly cleaning products that every home should have. Here was the first big intersection of hard work and Providence. Mr. Eggmeyer had been running a matching donation campaign that year for, get this, projects in Ethiopia being implemented by Living Water International! Out of 194 countries at that time and over 14,000 water charities it was more than a coincidence that we had picked precisely those two. We had raised $3,700 by that point and he matched the whole amount, increasing enthusiasm and driving momentum. Only $1,800 to go. By the end of 2011, we had raised over $10,000—more than the amount needed for the well in Ethiopia.

> *And with the first well overfunded, we thought "well we could do just one more."*

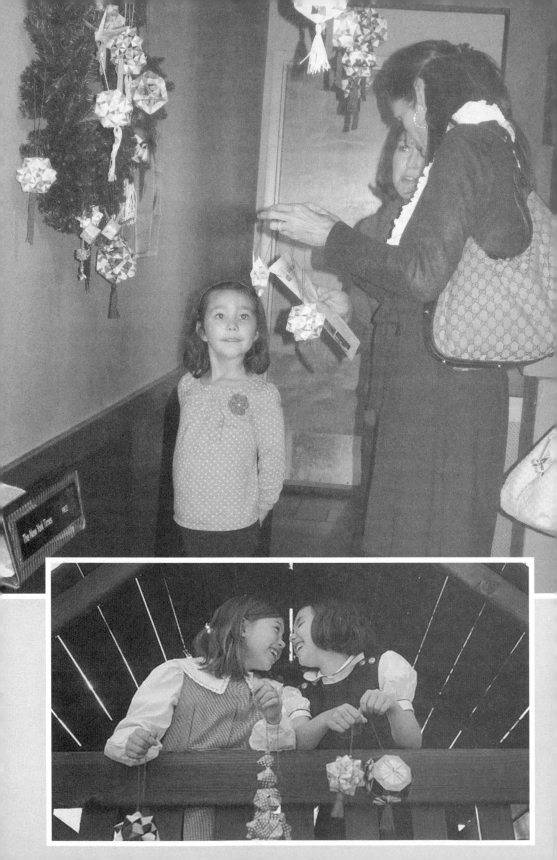

2012
JUST *ONE* MORE PROJECT

"Trust in the Lord with all your heart
and lean not on your own understanding;
in all your ways submit to him,
and he will make your paths straight."
Proverbs 3:5-6

Isabelle

Despite the fact that I was eight years old when this all started, the early years are a blur. Sometimes, I have to ask my parents how something happened, who was at that event, and why we were there.

From the beginning, if there was something that Katherine and I could do on our own or could be taught how to do with little time, we would do it. But there were still things that we weren't allowed to do, like driving ourselves to events. There were some things we didn't have the skills to do, like accounting and legal work. And then, there were some things our parents didn't want us to do, like manage our Facebook, Twitter, and Instagram accounts. They actually still don't, despite the fact that I'm now 18! Early on, I think they were concerned about creepy people having internet access to a five- and eight-year-old girl, but even as we've gotten older and more aware of what is inappropriate behavior, they've still kept us out of that arena and have paid people to handle it for us. I think they realized that social media can be a huge time sucker. **It's important and vital to what we do, but with all the homework and folding we had to do, it definitely needed to be outsourced.**

And then there were things our parents thought we could do that we didn't like to do and that even holds true today. If there was a thank-you card to write or a phone call to a donor to be made, we were the ones doing it. The excuse that my handwriting is terrible has never gotten me out of writing a single card. But that connection with our volunteers and donors has always paid off. People comment all the time and say, "I love what you're doing!"

And it's not just that we raise money to bring clean water and the Word to the thirsty, it's that we personally engage with all the people who give of their time and talents to our ministry. If there's a package to be delivered or a volunteer to be recognized at an awards event, Katherine and I are the ones doing it. We are the faces of **Paper For Water**. We know all our volunteers and major donors and love to interact with them. We also know that Paper for Water couldn't do what it does without them.

Now, I am a senior in high school, and not as goofy as I was back then, but Katherine and I are a magnet for parents who want to do something meaningful with their children.

• • •

Elevation Burger

Katherine

Paper for Water was a family affair, but our passion, love, and bubbly personalities kept bringing more amazing people into our lives. I look back on the videos and pictures of the early years and I can't help but think, *We were so stinking cute!*

By March, **Paper for Water** was still just a one-month project that kept getting additional months added on. There wasn't a written, strategic growth plan for the future. Katherine and I had no idea that our parents had a history of doing big, multi-year projects and that when they talked at night after we went to bed, they had an inkling that our project could turn into something big. We also wondered if there was another way to raise money besides all the time-consuming origami folding. That's why we decided to try something new.

The *Dallas Morning News* ran a full-color article about Paper for Water on the day of our first Elevation Burger fundraiser. Now, for those of you who don't know your burgers, Elevation Burger was a culinary delight! Grass-fed beef burgers cooked to perfection and served with just the right amount of lettuce and tomatoes (the correct

We know all our volunteers and major donors and love to interact with them. We also know that Paper for Water couldn't do what it does without them.

answer to the right amount is NONE) and served with melted cheese, toasted buns, and amazing French fries. But the really cool thing was that Elevation Burger had a give-back program. If you hosted an event at their restaurant, 10 percent of all dollars spent that day would be given to your organization.

One thing about that event that I still talk about to this day is a woman who had read the article in her morning paper. She drove to the restaurant and handed my mom a $20 dollar bill saying I don't like this kind of food, but I like what you are doing. She came solely to support our efforts!

After this, I was inside the restaurant playing with a friend when I noticed a well-dressed older lady enter Elevation Burger. She quickly scanned the restaurant but never looked up at the menu on the wall. It was pretty obvious she wasn't there to order. She briefly looked at me and then at Isabelle but didn't engage much beyond that as she looked at some of the other children too. I had a feeling she was looking for me, but I felt like she just didn't know if I was the person she was looking for. Then, she locked onto Mom and walked directly to her. She appeared to be a woman on a mission. She introduced herself, sat down, and started talking. Intrigued, I went and sat beside Mom.

Mom immediately smiled and introduced me to Mary Bloom. Mary smiled, and I was instantly drawn to her warmth and her charisma. She explained that she was the chief buyer for the Crow Collection of Asian Art's gift shop. She asked, "Have you ever been to the museum?

With my dad being half Japanese, of course, I responded, "Yes."

The Crow Collection was a cool place to visit downtown, and we'd been there often. My dad loved their samurai armor collection, and I loved the layout of the building and how there were lots of staircases that took you to different levels with secret seating areas and neat views of the people walking below. It always made me feel like a spy on a high-stakes mission scoping out my targets...but I digress.

Mary turned to my mom, "What would it take to convince you guys to come work with the Crow? Would you want to participate in the Family Days and host a table of origami folding? Maybe media exposure and part of the advertising for these events? Would Isabelle and Katherine be allowed to come tour the museum and see the underground private storage facilities for the museum? Would they like to meet the executive director, Amy Hofland, and maybe the son of the founders of the museum, Trammel Crow Jr.?"

Mary was hard selling my mom. I didn't know it at the time, but she was on a mission to make sure that we became part of the Crow Collection. She stayed and talked with us for about 30 minutes. Isabelle came over and Mom introduced her to Mary.

Isabelle loves museums for the art, not for the cool places to hide out and people-watch, so Mary and Isabelle actually had something to talk about. By the time Mary left, we'd made a verbal agreement to be part of the Crow Collection.

After she left, my mom laughed and said, "Mary had me at 'hello, I'm from the Crow Collection.'"

Now, I had seen my mom excited before, but this was definitely in the top five.

This new connection to the Crow Collection led us to an exciting meeting with the director, Amy Hofland, and the museum staff, where we were able to tell her our plans for solving the world water crisis and our dream to start up a volunteer club for kids to help us do just that. We can never thank Amy Hofland enough for all the ways she has supported us and believed in our ideas. We love her because she genuinely listened to all our ideas and then did her best to help us bring them into reality.

We've had a close family friend, "Uncle" Ron, who has been one of our staunchest supporters from the beginning. He was there that first night on November 3, and ten years later, he still comes to every folding event and volunteers weekly. He is an ever-present encouragement, donor, and volunteer.

"Uncle" Ron had a neighbor named Elaine Kollaja. Elaine occasionally wrote articles for the *Dallas Morning News,* and she was the person who had written the article the day of the Elevation Burger Fundraiser. Elaine also happened to be a talented CPA, and she had a lot of experience running a family foundation. The article and the fundraiser inspired her to help us reach the next important milestone of our journey. After our first interview with her, she asked us if we had thought about making **Paper for Water** an official nonprofit 501(c)3. "501(c)3?" I asked, "What the heck is that?"

Elaine laughed and explained, "It's a tax designation that the IRS grants to certain organizations so that people who donate money to you can get a tax deduction."

"Hmmm, that's interesting."

In my head, I was thinking, *Tax designation? IRS? What is she talking about?*

It turns out that my parents had been thinking about how to stop being a "pass-through" entity, and become a 501(c)3 so that they could apply for grants and have better access to our donors and connect with them directly. Apparently, Living Water's privacy rules prevented them from giving us detailed information on our donors. Our parents didn't explain that to us at the time, so while we sat through the conversation with Elaine, Isabelle and I were totally lost.

Shortly after that, Elaine became our first unpaid volunteer executive director and filed our paperwork to get our 501(c)3 designation. It was during a period that the US government was seriously scrutinizing nonprofits, so we thought it might take over a year to get our designation. Elaine was extremely detailed and plowed through page after required page submitting such a perfect application that we were approved in just over three months.

As Isabelle mentioned, our parents did the stuff behind the scenes that we couldn't do. Since my dad knew that once that 501(c)3 designation came through we would have to have a board of directors, he had a close group of fellow entrepreneurs that he tapped for recommendations. One of those people was a fellow doctor friend, Dr. Scott Conard, and another was a lawyer, Rugger Burke. They've both been hugely influential in the growth of our organization. Rugger put together our first policies and bylaws that were required when filing with the IRS. I still look at the document and am very grateful we had Rugger put that together because no one in our family had that skill set.

Dr. Scott Conard's early involvement brought the next person into our lives at precisely the right moment. Two months after he joined our board of directors, Dr. Conard introduced us to one of his collaborators, Diane Zuckerman. Diane was a member of the NYC Chapter of UN Women and was on the planning committee for the 2012 NYC UN Women's Chapter Sustainability Conference, which focused on female economic empowerment through energy, clean water, and immunizations. She invited us to be the kickoff speakers for the two-day event to be hosted in New York City!

We were kind of excited but seriously, what six- and eight-year-old really understand what the United Nations is? Or what it's like to stand up in front of hundreds of people and deliver a speech? If I was asked today to come back and speak, I would die from nerves, but we'd never been to New York City, let alone delivered a speech, so we didn't know we should be nervous.

Our dad sat us down and helped us prepare our speech. We spent hours and hours practicing. Our parents didn't want to freak us out, but it was the first time we'd traveled to speak somewhere and the first time we'd spoken in front of a large crowd of influential leaders. At that age, we didn't have a full grasp of the UN or the impact of the speech. I think we were more excited to skip school. Missing school was still fun and more of a treat rather than the pain an absence is today.

The morning of our event, Isabelle got up feeling pretty sick. It wasn't just nerves; she was honestly coming down with something. She'd never turn down a trip to a museum, but when it came time to tour the United Nations, Isabelle took a hard pass and stayed in the hotel sleeping. So Dad and I went to tour the UN. I don't remember a whole lot about it other than the pictures we have. I do remember the big hall where all the member nations meet to discuss world matters. I think Dad said something along the lines of, "Wouldn't it be cool if you got to represent the United States in this hall someday?" But my parents are always saying things like that.

We looked at a cool sculpture of a handgun with its barrel tied in a knot and another one of a machine gun that had been turned into a guitar. Then we walked down a hall with the UN's Sustainability & Development Goals (SDGs) on HUGE poster boards mounted to the wall. My dad pointed out SDGs four, five, and six that were in plain sight. Four was "quality education" – what we were doing was primarily so little girls like me could go to school and get an education. Five was "gender equality" – yup, right there, so little girls who were otherwise hauling water could go to school. And six was "clean water

& sanitation." Even at that age, I remember thinking that all these adults don't really understand. **Clean water needed to be #1 because you can't have "no poverty" (which is the first SDG) if you don't have clean water**. *At least it made the top 10 though.*

Funny enough, for my AP Human Geography class freshman year I held a 10-minute debate with one of my classmates about the most important SDG. Later I learned that he had actually volunteered with Paper for Water in the past and had simply just wanted to see if he could argue his way through and win. Naturally, I eventually won out, and when we presented our list of greatest needs to the class, Clean Water held the number-one spot.

After a delicious lunch at a little Italian restaurant by the UN, we made it back to the hotel only to find that Isabelle still felt pretty puny. We put on our matching green and black dresses, and after a quick stop at Starbucks, we hopped in a cab and drove to the auditorium hall of a large law firm. Isabelle perked up a bit when we arrived, and by the time we got on stage, she was ready to deliver.

Unfortunately, I delivered my awesome line, "Even though my dad's a doctor, I've saved more lives than he has this year," so quietly that I'm not sure that anyone heard it.

My dad had coached me that there was going to be a laugh after that, but there wasn't. Isabelle started with her next line, "Even though I'm not a minister, I've helped spread the Good News. And even though I don't have a degree in public health, I've helped stop the spread of some diseases."

We had a little breakdown in our speech, and I had to whisper Isabelle's line to her, but we didn't quit, didn't freak out, and finished up.

When the crowd leaped to their feet to give us our first standing ovation, the applause validated and reinforced the idea that there were people interested in what we were doing outside of our community—not our friends, not our family, but people who had no connection to us beforehand.

With a deeper understanding and respect, I wish I could go back because I would be really interested in hearing the other speakers now and touring the UN again. So, if someone from the UN reads this book, please invite us back!

• • •

Good Morning Texas

Isabelle

By this point, the *Dallas Morning News*, the local White Rock newspaper, and a local magazine called *The Advocate* had featured us in their publications. Sometime in early September of 2012, we received a call from WFAA, which is the ABC affiliate in Dallas, about their program *Good Morning Texas*, a daily morning show that mimics the *Good Morning America* format.

The show's producers said, "We want to do a piece on **Paper for Water.** Would you be interested?"

Would we be interested?! Were they crazy? We'd never been on TV before. This idea was AMAZING! And to top it all off, we were going to get to miss school! A few months prior, our parents had approached our school headmaster, Dr. Jeffrey, about another event that required us to miss some school. Dr. Jeffrey expressed excitement for us and said, "As long as the girls are wearing their school uniforms during school hours, they can raise money for water and the Word to be delivered to developing countries."

Katherine and I had laughed at the time, thinking, "*Oh, he probably just wants it to be easy for us to get to class quickly and not have to change clothes in the minivan on the way to school.*" But we quickly learned that we weren't being introduced as "two girls from Dallas" but rather "two girls from Providence Christian School of Texas." We still laugh about Dr. Jeffrey's "genius Providence PR."

On the morning of September 7, 2012, Katherine and I woke up extra early with our parents and drove to the WFAA studios in the central courtyard of the American Airlines Center. If you've never been there, it's an amazing building complex with shiny chrome everywhere, fancy restaurants, and lots of glass windows. Since you can see into the studios from outside, people will often line up behind barriers to look in on the studios as they're recording programs.

On the morning of our segment, they were also filming an interview with some comedian and movie star that we'd never heard of, Rob Schneider. Apparently, he was a big deal because my dad seemed to get all excited when the lady who met us in the lobby told us that he was going to be on stage before we were.

I'm not sure if you've picked up on this yet, but Katherine and I are pretty much "rule followers." Since I'm the oldest, rules are pretty important to me. Katherine's just a good kid and rarely rocks the boat, but our youngest sister, Trinity… not so much.

Since the plan was to drop her at ballet after we had finished recording and been dropped off at school, she'd worn her ballerina tights and leotard to the studio. She had woken up that morning repeating the mantra, "I'm a lion. I'm a lion. I'm a lion" and crawled on all fours at our house roaring like a lion whenever she had a chance. At one point, my dad asked her to stop, and she replied, "I can't! I'm a lion!"

So imagine that "hot mess" tagging along with you into a TV studio where everyone is supposed to be quiet when the red "ON AIR" sign goes on. And then imagine when the red light goes off having a 3-year-old in her pink ballerina outfit jumping onto the stage furniture and roaring like a lion. Luckily, the hosts of *Good Morning Texas* thought it was pretty funny and cute but not me. I was mortified! It did nothing for my nervousness as I was about to go on TV for the first time in my life.

Fortunately, though, Amy Hofland, the Executive Director of the Crow Collection of Asian Art, was also there for the segment. We'd done a couple of Saturday events at the Crow Collection, and she was helping us put together a December trunk show where we could exchange our ornaments for donations. Amy, who was awesome to work with, really helped put me at ease.

Amy and Mom helped us set up our table of ornaments using beautiful obis, the sash part of a kimono that is made of silk and often brightly colored, while Dad tried to keep Trinity corralled and quiet. After the setup, Amy stood just off-camera as Carrie McClure began to interview us and then joined us on camera halfway through the interview.

It's so funny to look back at that video from nine years ago and see just how short and how unprepared we were for the questions that Carrie asked. Oh my gosh, we were so tiny, cute, and shy! We still laugh watching the video and seeing Katherine yawn every few minutes. Remember we arrived really early that day and she was only 6.

Just after we finished on set, Carrie ran over to another stage. The studio audience started cheering for Rob Schneider as soon as he came out on stage. When he sat down and pointed across the studio at us exiting our set, he asked Carrie, "Who are those cute kids over there?"

Suddenly, we were in the spotlight again, and this time with no warning, no preparation, and no idea what to say. While on live TV, Rob gave us a $40 donation and asked me to pick out my favorite ornament. Just as I was about to give him the ornament I'd selected, I realized that it was a $60 ornament. I quickly put it back in the box of ornaments and found a $40 one to give him. I didn't care if he was super famous. Each of those ornaments took over an hour to make and he wasn't about to get some kind of "celebrity deal" from me.

Since that day in 2012, Katherine and I have been back at least twice for *Good Morning Texas* and have also had the privilege of being guests on other TV shows like *Good Morning America, Texas Country Reporter*, and other TV channels like Nickelodeon and The Disney Channel.

Over the years, Katherine and I have had the opportunity to meet a number of actors, and somewhere along the line, concluded that being famous celebrities is not for us. Paper for Water has never been about us getting famous. From very early on, my mom would always remind us that we were striving to put the fame and spotlight on those in need living in developing countries who don't have access to clean water. When giving speeches and being interviewed, we would always think about all the kids we were representing who couldn't afford a plane ticket to come and advocate for themselves.

The morning of the *Good Morning Texas* interview Marylee and James Labar happened to be tuned in for the show. Something we said moved them to want to help and they called their daughter, Jamie Labar, and asked her to help us. Jamie, an artist and showroom designer and owner of an art gallery called LuminArte, sent us an email that day and my mom called back to set up a meeting at her beautiful gallery after school. We walked into her Dallas Design District gallery and immediately loved everything about it. Gorgeous artwork was hung throughout the well-lit rooms. What we didn't know was that Jamie hadn't seen the news piece and didn't actually know anything about Paper for Water. Luckily we had brought a box of ornaments and a photo book highlighting what we were doing to help people get clean water. Jamie listened to our presentation and then took us under her wing setting up an art show and origami folding event for us. She introduced us to a lot more people and our circle grew. We are grateful that she listened to her parents' plea to help us and so generously did just that. We were learning that every action we took led to someone or something else. Sometimes results were immediate and sometimes we were planting seeds that we wouldn't see grow till years later.

Good Morning Texas

• • •

Our First Awards

Isabelle

In the fall of 2012, we received **The Each Moment Matters Award** and **The Dallas Association of Fundraising Professionals' Youth in Philanthropy Award.**

The AFP award—a massive beautiful blue glass sculpture—is hands-down the coolest we've ever gotten. It was so heavy that Katherine and I could barely carry it. Size-wise, it's probably the biggest award we've ever received. For years, it rested on the middle of the mantel in our living room and now is in the **Paper for Water** *office. The award is still super special to us as a symbol and nod to the start of this journey.*

Winning these awards not only encouraged our efforts but connected us to new people and opportunities. One of these was our first unscripted, on-stage interview at the Association of Fundraising Professionals DFW Philanthropy Conference.

Even though I'd have my sister with me for the interview panel, the idea of making up responses on the spot made me nervous. I think we both felt anxious because up until this moment, everything we'd done was very well-rehearsed, completely memorized speeches.

On the day of the event, we changed outfits numerous times, focusing on and planning every other detail that was within our control. I also have a distinct memory of stopping at CVS and buying orange nail polish to match my dress. Painting my nails helped distract me a little from the nervousness, but as I traced over the nail bed, I ran over sample questions in my mind. *What would the moderator ask me? What stories do I want to tell?*

After walking into the lights and onto the stage, time zipped by. We actually met and shared the stage with another kid our age and fellow winner of the Fort Worth club award, Will Lourcey. Meeting Will, the founder of FROGS (friends reaching our goals), an organization focused on feeding those in need, inspired us and broadened our network, showing us that there were other service-oriented kids like us. We kept in touch with him for a few years, and every now and then, we still see him at other events.

Holly Hull Miori was another important connection we made due to these two awards. There are few people with a heart for others as big as Holly's. She was the person who nominated us for the AFP and then facilitated our participation in this conference. She was one of our first board members and has helped and advised us countless times over the years.

• • •

Yahoo Finance Article

Katherine

While social media is definitely one of the ways in which we try to leverage our message, we have never really figured out how to make things go viral. We've done a ton of videos, and we've tried to increase our followers and subscribers through different marketing campaigns. And yet as of 2021, we still hover under 10,000 followers on Facebook, just over 1,000 subscribers on YouTube, under 900 followers on Twitter, and under 5,000 followers on Instagram.

Oprah hasn't had us on her TV show. We still haven't monetized our YouTube channel, but I will also remind you that **Paper for Water** started five years before TikTok was even founded, the same year that Snapchat was founded and only one year after Instagram posted its first photo.

In those early years though, we did have one instance where we thought that the whole world might hear about us and that was shortly after one of our neighbors, Chris Nichols, learned about our mission. Chris was a writer for *Yahoo Finance* and covered interesting topics like the London Stock Exchange and how this crazy thing called Bitcoin had jumped from $1 to $32 in 6 short months in 2011. (Now, I wish we'd invested all the donations received in 2011 into Bitcoin! We would have had $640,000,000 in May of 2021!) Anyway, coming to our house to interview Isabelle, Mom, and me, he put together a write-up of our project to publish on the internet on December 19, 2012.

I'm pretty sure my parents didn't know that it had been published that day because my dad called us while we were at the grocery store and excitedly said, "We just went from 1,000 followers on Facebook to 2,000 in the last two hours!"

It had taken us months to accumulate those first 1,000 followers, and suddenly in the span of two hours, we had doubled. Dad was sure that our PayPal account was going to start exploding with donations and kept checking the balance every fifteen minutes or so. But, that morning's starting balance of $152 remained at $152 for the whole day. Eventually, Dad figured out that the Yahoo article was the source of all the new followers on Facebook. The initial onslaught of new followers slowed, and by dinner time, our account was easily over 3,000 followers but our PayPal balance was still sitting at $152.

Over the next few weeks, our follower number climbed into the high 3,000 range, but you guessed it, the PayPal account remained at $152. The comments gave us a special kind of currency though because we received 56 typed pages of positive comments.

I am not a social media expert, but I've been told by a number of social media experts to never read the comments when something is posted about yourself. Over the years, I saw how people continued to love hearing our story. I have found that 97 percent of the time, people love to hear "feel good" stories about kids doing things. It makes them feel better about the future and helps them believe that the world will be in good hands.

• • •

$50,000 Goal

Isabelle

> *All children have the heart to help, and kids have no limits on what they think they can achieve. It's later as we go through life that we place ourselves in boxes and create limitations. So at that age, the experience at the UN encouraged us and spurred the idea to fund ten water projects by the end of the year, which meant we would have to raise $50,000. At that point,* **Paper for Water** *was tiny. It had been nine months since we'd started, and we'd only raised around $20,000.*

At a family planning session that August, my parents asked, "What kind of goals do you have for the rest of the year?"

"I want us to raise $50,000 by the end of December," I said.

Both of my parents shot down the idea pretty quickly. My dad grabbed a legal pad and penciled in some calculations, "If you want to build enough origami to raise $50,000, you need 37,000 sheets of paper. You'll need to fold 20 hours per day and are going to have to drop out of school. This is not a realistic goal."

Their response went against what everyone had told us up to that point, "You can do whatever you want," "Dream big," "The sky's the limit." So when my rather outrageous goal met the "No, you can't do that, it's not possible," I was frankly crushed. But the next morning, my mom was doing her Bible study and it was all about doing whatever you are afraid of or think is impossible and letting God take care of whatever you can't. She felt moved to come downstairs and read it all again to us. When she finished, I told her, "You and Dad don't think that God can handle this." She was convicted by the truth of what she'd read and by what we said.

Amazingly, within two hours, my mom received an email from a mom who wanted to volunteer with her daughter. This was the first time a non-family member offered to help. This opened a whole new level of possibilities as we were no longer the only ones folding. We brought on friends and church members, and the growth exploded from there. Soon we were hosting origami folding parties at our home. The light bulb had gone off and we now knew how we could get those 37,000 pieces of paper folded *without* quitting school.

My dad reached back out to Curtis Eggemeyer, who had given us our first matching donation back in 2011. Curtis was excited to hear that we were still fundraising and he offered a matching donation for up to $50,000! Dad was probably most excited and said, "This is fantastic! Now we only need to raise $25,000 to meet our goal."

I protested, "No, he's offering $50,000. We're going to get all $50,000." Launching into the fall and a chaotic season with our new mission, we attended Christmas fairs, gift markets, and art galleries. By mid-December, I stood at a craft fair in Richardson asking people, "Have you heard about **Paper for Water**?"

We were so close to our goal. If we had a good day at the market, we knew we could reach it. I marked a sheet of paper to keep a running tally of the sales and thanked buyers for helping us reach our goal. A couple of dollars beyond our target, the emcee announced over the PA system, "**Paper for Water** has officially reached their goal in raising $50,000 for the global water crisis."

Katherine and I started jumping up and down. Mom started crying. The whole crowd cheered. It was a meaningful moment of community celebration and proof that we really could set and achieve Big Dream goals. I realized we could achieve whatever we set our minds to. The success validated the dream-big mentality and demonstrated that kids' ideas matter, that we have a less limited mindset and that adults aren't always right. It showed me, and probably Katherine too, that we had ideas worth pursuing and maybe we were capable of a bit more than adults thought they could achieve themselves. That's a pretty big thing to realize when you're a 10-year-old.

"We did it. We did it," I said.

And we still had a few weeks left till the end of the year.

2013
BUILDING MOMENTUM

"What you get by achieving your goals is not as important as what you become by achieving your goals."
Henry David Thoreau

2013 was so busy it was crazy. We had gotten pretty busy folding paper and speaking at little gigs like weekly Rotary meetings and church youth groups and of course participating in the monthly Family Day events at the Crow. We added additional gift markets to our schedule and a new favorite, teaching origami at the Hilton Anatole's Holiday Sparkle event in exchange for free skating for us and all our participating volunteers. Some of the biggest highlights of 2013 included doing an interview for Chevy Hometown Kids, receiving the Chiapas International Women's Foundation Award for Women Who Bring Hope, being featured in the American Girl magazine, and the Harry Westmoreland Lifetime Achievement Award.

Katherine
Alright, I need to come clean. We've alluded to it and put in a couple of Bible verses and hinted at our Christianity, but it would be a disservice to our readers if we didn't put it out there. My sister and I are atypical

Gen Z in that we don't have social media. We're normal Gen Z in that we believe in diversity and inclusion.

We don't want to alienate anyone that isn't Christian because we have amazing, dedicated volunteers of all faiths. Showing the love of Jesus means just that, love—love for all people—and we do our best to make everyone feel welcome. At all of our water projects around the world, everyone is welcome to get clean water regardless of faith *but* we strongly believe God's hand has been on this project since its inception, and its inception truly started long before we were even born.

I mean, what better parents to have behind the scenes than ours, the crazy dad, doctor entrepreneur, and the grounded, operational overthinker mom? Both of them have hearts for the underserved and

God's hand has been on this project since its inception,

the desire to leave this world a better place. They committed to making sure that when we leave their house, we are independent young adults capable of successfully being on our own.

Even from the beginning with the story about Curtis Eggemeyer only wanting to match funds for LWI wells in Ethiopia, there have been definite experiences that can't be attributed to serendipity or chance. Sometimes these miraculous things seem to happen almost daily. My mom often says that she can't wait to get up and see what miracle will happen today.

Not only have we had an opportunity to experience magical moments, but we've learned that philanthropy and volunteer work don't just feel good, they can also be a lot of fun. Like when we met Dallas icon, and lovely lady, Ebby Halliday on her 103rd birthday.

Building Momentum

My dad knew some of the leaders at Communities Foundation of Texas and learned that Ebby was being inducted into the Entrepreneurs' Hall of Fame on her 103rd birthday. He volunteered us to make a large table-top ornament as a present to be given to her on stage.

At that same event, we met Garrett Boone, CEO for The Container Store, and my dad bid on a lunch with him in the silent auction. Through the scheduling of that lunch, we met Mr. Boone's executive assistant, Karla Buie, who joined our board of directors and introduced us to Hedda Dowd, the founder of the restaurant, rise no.1, who then introduced us to Karen Katz, the CEO for Neiman Marcus, who helped guide us through the process of getting a Fantasy Gift in the Neiman Marcus catalog—a fully decorated Christmas tree that sold for $50,000. But I should probably slow down as I just gave you a preview of four years of work and connections. And all I wanted to do was tell you about a birthday party for Ebby.

After Ebby received our ornament, the organizers arranged for everyone to have a photo with her. There were literally hundreds of Dallas CEOs and executives at this event, and we got in line with all of them to have our picture taken with this lady we hardly knew. Our dad was in line with us, which was fortunate because I'm sure you can imagine how exciting it was to stand in line for 45 minutes to get a picture with someone we didn't even know.

Dad whispered, "H. Ross Perot is in line immediately behind us."

Who? I didn't have a clue who he was. Dad seemed to have been a little star-struck, but he spoke for a few moments with Mr. Perot before turning back to entertain us.

Our turn for the photo came, and we sat on either side of Mrs. Halliday. She looked down at us a little surprised and said, "Are you the **Paper for Water** girls?"

Isabelle giggled and said shyly, "Yes, ma'am."

Mrs. Halliday immediately clapped her hands, which quieted the room and said, "Alright everyone, leave us."

This created quite a stir, but she waved people toward the door. The photographer looked at her and said, "Ummm, do you want me to leave?"

"Yes," said Ebby.

Our dad stayed around, and Mrs. Halliday looked at him before asking, "Who are you, sir?"

He replied, "I'm their father."

Ebby said, "Well, you should definitely leave for a few minutes while I speak with your wonderful daughters."

Mr. Perot with his deep Texas drawl said, "You don't mean me too, Ms. Ebby, do ya?"

She laughed and waved H. Ross Perot out of the room before proceeding to talk with us as if she were our best friend. She asked us about school, and she asked us about our project and why we were doing what we were doing. And then, she asked us a question that no one had ever asked us, "Are you doing this whole thing, or are your parents doing it?"

Isabelle found her voice first and responded, "No ma'am. Our parents do help because we can't drive, and we need to get places, but we are doing this so girls our age in developing countries can go to school."

I piped up and said, "And so little kids like our sister Trinity don't die because they're drinking dirty water."

Ebby smiled and wiped away a tear, "Well, keep doing what you're doing and if you ever feel like it's not you driving this project, you can say, 'No.'"

How many people at their own birthday party would be willing to take ten minutes out of their celebration to reinforce two little girls' autonomy and ability to self-direct?

Meeting Ebby Halliday seemed to be just a part of the path the Great Strategist was laying down to help us grow **Paper for Water.**

• • •

Isabelle

As Katherine mentioned, Ebby's serendipitous event seemed like it could only be divinely orchestrated, as it led to multiple connections and opportunities. After winning the lunch with Garrett Boone at the silent auction, my dad called to set up the time and day. This was a big opportunity for us to get in front of someone who had grown a small furniture business into an organizing empire. We were excited to see what we could learn.

After we'd arrived at The Container Store headquarters, a massive, huge building, and walked in the door, the employees greeted us, "Oh my gosh, it's the **Paper for Water** girls. We're so excited to meet you!"

Blown away that people knew who we were, I thought, *Wow, this is awesome!* We met up with Mr. Boone at a super fancy cafeteria in their

"Well, keep doing what you're doing and if you ever feel like it's not you driving this project, you can say, 'No.'"

headquarters, but it was definitely a different type of cafeteria than I'd ever been to, more like a restaurant. Then came the free stuff. It may sound a bit strange for a kid to be excited about office supplies, but these bags were full of awesome Post-its and papers, practical items that we really needed. Katherine and I also each received a Container Store lunch box, and I swear we used those things every day for six or seven years. We used them until we wore them out and still keep one of them for whenever Trinity misplaces her lunch box, which is often.

After receiving our goodie bags, we toured the office and got to see the giant warehouse. It was really fun, and I thought it was cool how we were able to see the inner workings of such a big company. I was amazed that Mr. Boone knew the name of every single employee that we passed by. Not only did he know everyone's name, but we could tell he knew each person well from the personal questions he asked when he greeted them. While on-site, we met Karla Buie, Mr. Boone's personal assistant at the time, and talked with her for a while. She really loved what we were doing, and she asked, "Is there any way I can get involved?"

We ended up asking her to be on our board of directors, where she served for a couple of years before moving out of state. While she was on the board, she was super amazing and helped us so much. She is one of the kindest and most positive people I know. But before I get ahead of myself, back to The Container Store meeting. Before we left that day, we were invited to the grand opening of a new store. Obviously, we said, yes: there was no way we were going to turn that down.

So we went to a giant party for the new store and witnessed the power of The Container Store brand. Outside of the dancing and eating, the event was awesome and it was great just to have some fun. Since then, we've been blessed to partner with The Container Store in various ways. You may have even seen a photo of one of our origami Christmas ornaments tucked in an ornament storage box in a Christmas catalog. They have given us beautiful paper and supplies and stepped up to help us when our office was flooded in the 2021 snowstorm that we refer to as Snowmaggedon.

In the spring, Elaine Kollaja arranged for us to participate in SMU's Engineering and Humanities Week and to make the table decorations for its fundraiser dinner. The morning before the fundraiser we had a chance to do an interview for Chevy Hometown Kids and see a project on display at Fair Park, The Plastiki. The Plastiki was a take on the famous Contiki, but the 60-foot catamaran was made entirely from 12,500 recycled plastic bottles and other recycled PET plastic waste products!

Some of the boat's crew were on-site to answer questions about their well-documented journey from San Francisco, California, to Sydney,

Australia. A documentary featured how they built the vessel and then captured the four-month, 8,000-mile voyage between the two cities. I thought it was pretty incredible that they crossed the whole Pacific on this tiny boat made of plastic water bottles and chatted with them about recycling and the importance of not dumping plastic water bottles.

The Plastiki's efforts were to give a voice to the ocean and its marine life suffering from massive plastic gyres. Some we learned were as large as the state of Texas! It was very similar to how **Paper for Water** tries to give a voice to those without clean water. Because of this, their mission resonated with mine. When I think of the overuse of plastic water bottles, it makes me a bit sad and angry. Katherine and I have always used reusable water bottles, and I don't think people consider how the effects of a small decision such as that can make a huge impact. Most people don't realize that it takes almost three times as much water to create a plastic water bottle as the amount of water that bottle can hold. What a waste of clean water! If each person made one small change, the ripple effects of the change would add up collectively.

Chevy Hometown Kids Episode

• • •

After School Awards

Isabelle

Remember Mrs. Thornhill, my first-grade teacher who supported us from our very first event? Well, she nominated us for the After School Awards. This was a very different award than the ones we had won previously as the winner was decided by a social media vote. Honestly, the odds of winning didn't seem to be in our favor, but the $5,000 awarded to the winner was a huge sum then and sure motivated me to do everything in my power to win this popularity contest. At the time, we hadn't been doing **Paper for Water** very long and didn't have much of a social media base. The competition was also pretty fierce and actually reconnected us with Will, our friend and fellow winner of AFP's Youth in Philanthropy Award. He set an awesome example and had been running his charity longer, but of course, I still wanted to win! Katherine and I concluded that if we lost, it wouldn't be due to lack of effort and decided to ask everyone we met to vote for us.

If each person made one small change, the ripple effects of the change would add up collectively.

During the five-month stretch the contest ran, we flew to Las Vegas with our family to visit the Grand Canyon with some relatives from Japan. Not only were we going to continue our daily social media posts and email nudges, but also before leaving for the trip, Katherine and I cut little slips of paper out with scissors that included voting instructions.

On the flight, I told the flight attendant about our mission and asked her if she'd help us win the contest by voting for us.

"And you can vote every day," I said.

When we were landing, she went a step above and beyond and made an announcement on the plane.

"Attention passengers, we have two special girls on board who need your help to win a contest that will benefit their charity, **Paper for**

Water. It's the last week of the contest and every vote brings them closer to winning $5,000 that will help fund water projects. We are still taxiing to the gate, so please do these young ladies a favor and vote at afterschoolawards.com." (unfortunately now a defunct website).

As soon as she got off the intercom, everyone around us pulled out their phones. This added some fuel and excitement to our mission. Once we deplaned, Katherine and I ran to every rental car counter. As she handed our homemade business card to the agent, I'd ask for their vote.

During that last week, we went on a voting blitz. If you were on an elevator visiting the Hoover Dam or the Grand Canyon at the same time as us, you would've likely received that slip of paper with voting instructions and details on our mission.

A couple of weeks later while shopping, Katherine and I were trying on clothes in a dressing room when I heard a shriek from my mom. I peeked outside the door to find my mom smiling and crying.

"You won," she said. "You guys aren't going to believe it, but you won!"

Ecstatic, Katherine and I started jumping up and down. I honestly couldn't believe it and needed to read the email for myself.

> *I think the experience showed us that when you dedicate yourself to hard work and are persistent, big things can happen. It also demonstrated how collective and consistent grassroots action can pay off. We didn't have that much experience. We hadn't been involved with the philanthropy project that long. Our following wasn't as large as some of the other nominees. We just worked harder.*

Looking back, this event supports the idea that kids can accomplish incredible things and that they can even do more than adults. If our mom had walked up to the flight attendant and tried to convince her to vote, she may have voted, but would she have gotten on the intercom to announce to the entire plane? I don't think so. There are great advantages to being young.

And I love thinking of the possibilities for each of those short encounters! We were able to touch so many people by going past fear or hesitation. Over the years, one of the things that helped me approach strangers or speak on stages has been knowing how much I needed to be brave and speak on behalf of other kids, the ones who can't afford a plane ticket to speak on their own behalf, the ones who are carrying water for miles to their village. That still gives me courage today.

Dear Volunteers, donors, supporters, and prayer warriors,
We thank you very much for helping us bring clean water and the word to the thirsty in 2012. With your help were able to raise $117,417 and bring clean water to 23 communities in India. We could never have done it without you!

We would like to announce our 2013 goal.

5 wells in Kenya	$60,000
7 wells in Ghana	$84,000
5 wells in Liberia	$75,000
6 wells in India	$30,000

Reaching this goal means transforming thousands of lives. If you would like to help us or learn more about the thirsty please email us at paperforwater@hotmail.com.

God bless you,
Isabelle and Katherine
Paper for Water

The Harry Westmoreland Lifetime Achievement Award & Living Water Galas

Katherine

Sometime in the late summer of 2013, Dad got a call from a Living Water International Board Member, Jack Vaughn. Mr. Vaughn was the CEO of an oil and gas company called Vaughn Energy. Dad didn't know him personally but knew of his philanthropic heart and had met him several times at charity fundraisers across Texas. I was sitting next to Dad when he got the call, and I think he was a little taken by surprise that Mr. Vaughn would be calling him. I could only hear Dad's side of the conversation and I couldn't figure out what was going on.

"Mr. Vaughn, good to hear your voice…oh, yes, sorry, Jack…But they've only been doing this for two years…Yes, I don't doubt that the board has prayed about this. Oh, yes, I know the girls have been working hard but I just don't think… No, I can understand that ALL the board members have prayed about this… Well, of course, we wouldn't want to do that. Yes, of course, they'll accept it….Yes, I will let the girls know… Yes, we'll be there in person…Yes, thank you so much for this honor. God bless you too. Goodbye."

I don't see Dad cry very often, but he started tearing up. Mom immediately became concerned, "Is everything OK?" she asked.

"Do you remember Jack Vaughn? From the board of directors of Living Water International? He just turned 70 and has been volunteering for LWI now for twenty years. Remember how last year he was awarded the Harry Westmoreland Lifetime Achievement Award from LWI? Harry Westmoreland was one of the founders of LWI, who passed away several years ago. The Lifetime Achievement Award has been given to a US senator, the president of Kenya, CEOs of several companies, and now LWI wants to give it to Isabelle and Katherine!"

We all sat there a little stunned and speechless. I was shocked. It was the highest award you can receive at the Living Water Gala and had been awarded to people who have dedicated their entire lives to helping people—people who have been working at it tirelessly for decades.

Mom spoke up first, "But, they've only been doing this for two years. Jack has been volunteering for twenty years!"

"That's what I told him, but he responded that he was seventy and had been doing this since he was fifty. He said Katherine is seven and has been doing this since she was five. So it was the same percentage of life span." Dad smiled and laughed before continuing, "Jack said that all the board members had prayed about this, and they thought it was the right thing to do, that it would inspire not just other kids but all the adults who attend the annual Gala. What was I supposed to say other than, 'Of course they'll accept'?"

I think my parents had been planning on going to the Gala anyway, but now we suddenly had to plan a speech and buy party clothes. We spent hours and hours practicing for the speech. I practiced in the car, in the living room, and while getting dressed in the morning. Even though I knew all the information like the back of my hand, I wanted to memorize the speech word for word. I didn't trust my ability to not freeze up, and there was no way I could come up with something on the spot. Dad printed off our speeches and highlighted our parts in green and pink. He'd helped us by placing extended spaces on the piece of paper when I needed to pause, and by typing, "smile here' or "slow down."

On the day of the event, we arrived early and were shown to the Green Room. It's funny that even at seven, I knew what a Green Room was and wasn't surprised to find glasses, ice, Sprite, Coke, and snacks to munch on as we waited for our rehearsal. Once we'd finished that, we chatted with Mega Donors at their happy hour before being rushed back to the Green Room to wait for about 20 minutes.

When I look back at the videos, I still can't believe I was only seven years old when Isabelle and I walked out onto a stage in front of 1,500 people in a huge ballroom and delivered a speech. I don't remember everything, but I've watched the video enough to know our speech by heart:

Isabelle: "We began taking donations for origami creations on November 3, 2011. Since then, we have raised over $176,000 for clean water. What we want to share with you today are some of the things we've learned on this adventure."

Me: "We've learned that you can do anything with God, even that which seems impossible."

Isabelle: "We've learned to trust the Lord and believe in Him."

Me: "Prayer is powerful."

Isabelle: "We've learned not to give up."

Me: "We've learned that when you give a lot, you get a lot back, and sometimes you get more than you gave."

Isabelle: "We've learned that a lot of people don't even know about the world water crisis. But when you tell them, they are anxious to help."

Me: "We've learned that everyone wants to make a difference in the world. God uses all people young and old to make the world a better place."

Isabelle: "If everyone in this world helps a little, it all adds up to a lot."

Me: "We are called to be God's tools, putting the fame and spotlight on those in need rather than ourselves."

Isabelle: "Take one small step and then another, you never know where you might end up. Millions have lived without love but none without water. But with Living Water International, no one has to live without water or the love of Jesus."

Isabelle and Katherine: "Won't you join us?"

At that point, the room erupted in applause and Mike Mantel, the CEO for LWI walked out on stage and said, "Hello, Madams CEOs." And we responded in the way we still address Mike when we see him, "Hellooooo, Mister C.E.O."

Mike addressed the crowd and asked for nine more leaders like us to help them meet their fundraising goals for 2013, and by the end of the evening, we learned that LWI had raised almost $3,000,000.

The Harry Westmoreland Lifetime Achievement Award now has a very prominent location on the bookshelf in our offices. It is a daily reminder that we are on a mission to solve the world water crisis. Our work is not done yet, even though I've been working on **Paper for Water** now for over 66 percent of my life and Isabelle for 59 percent.

Perseverance, grit, and persistence are all things that we talk about when we speak to youth about the world water crisis. Nothing we've accomplished has happened overnight. Sometimes people that we met four or five years earlier reappear in our lives in ways we could never have imagined and suddenly have something big to offer us. If we had decided to quit after the first six months or even after the first five years, we wouldn't have been able to see how God works in mysterious ways.

Ever since winning the Harry Westmoreland Award and attending that event, the LWI Gala has become one of my favorite events. It's always toward the beginning of the school year, which is the start of our busiest season. Every year, I leave energized by the people and the stories of how we are changing people's lives. It's a great reminder of why we do what we do and an awesome way to kick off the crazy fundraising season! We also have some great stories from these galas, so if you ever talk to me in person after reading this book, make sure to ask about a certain elevator ride at 5:30 in the morning on the way to Hobby International Airport to get to school...

Harry Westmoreland Award

• • •

Inspired to Continue

Isabelle

After funding 23 wells in India, Dad started talking with Shannon Strossner, the Living Water International (LWI) representative who lived in Houston and had been assigned to us. Shannon and Dad had been discussing how Katherine and I were getting tired. Lots of folding, lots of events, lots of late nights. Dad thought we needed something to reinspire us. Shannon informed Dad that because of liability insurance issues, we were too young to go on a well-drilling trip with LWI but that we could probably put a trip to India together to go visit some of our water projects. Because our personal overarching goal was to help girls go to and stay in school, most of these wells were located at schools.

Working with the LWI representatives, Mom and Dad put together a plan to go to India during our 2013 Christmas vacation. Mom invited Grandma and Papa Watters to join us, and it sounded super fun. Katherine and I had talked about it in our bunk beds, "How was Santa Claus going to find us in India?!"

As I would later learn, the week or so leading up to a major trip is always *crazy*! Dad was worried that we wouldn't eat any of the food on our trip, so he'd bought Power Bars, beef jerky, and other things that wouldn't spoil and would provide us with protein. We didn't eat nearly as much of our backup snacks as we thought we would, because we discovered naan! Buttered naan, garlic naan, chicken tandoori and naan, plain naan! Yes, we learned that some spicy Indian food is like sticking a hot iron poker in your mouth, but for the most part, we survived our food adventures. (If you run into our Papa, ask him about the fresh tomatoes he ate toward the end of our trip.)

We left the US on the twenty-first of December and flew through Dubai to New Delhi. There, we checked into a palatial hotel to get oriented and spend the twenty-second and twenty-third driving around Delhi visiting tombs and temples and eating amazing food at hotels that had been built during the British Empire's occupation of India. I'm not sure that we've ever stayed in nicer hotels. But the dichotomy between the wealthy and the poor wasn't just uncomfortable as it is here in the US when you walk out of a nice restaurant and see an elderly person on a street corner begging, it was jarring and painful. There were so many homeless children, some with leprosy, and whole families living in cardboard structures. It wasn't unusual to see little babies sleeping on the ground next to a major road sometimes unattended but often with their mothers right next to them cooking food in an empty can over a small fire. I wasn't prepared for that. Katherine and I asked a lot of questions, "Who is taking care of that baby? Why is the child pooping on the sidewalk? Do these kids get to go to school?"

We drove three hours to Agra and checked into our hotel on Christmas Eve. We walked around the stalls of local craftsmen and tried on beautiful silk saris. My Papa purchased a beautiful inlaid marble table that he still has in his living room. When he had it shipped back to the US with some carpets, it took months to show up!

The next morning, when my sisters and I woke up to Santa presents of Indian elephant purses, I thought, *Hmmm, apparently Santa makes use of local goods but where are my Legos that I asked for?*

Afterward, we ate a yummy breakfast of what the waiters called donuts, but let me reassure you, these were no Krispy Kremes. We then spent the morning walking around the Taj Mahal where we were able to take some amazing pictures. It was so much more beautiful than any photo I'd ever seen. The stone actually glitters. I remember Dad commenting about how unique this Christmas was and saying, "Here we are a Christian family celebrating Christmas at breakfast and then touring a Muslim mosque dedicated to the wife of a dead emperor."

I love that about my parents. They are pretty solid in their faith, but they definitely expose us to the world so that we can learn how others around us live.

On the twenty-sixth, we drove seven hours to Lucknow to meet up with Shannon, who had flown all the way from Texas to join us on the tour of our water projects. My dad had also paid to bring a professional videographer along with us, Doug. Doug "the Bug" was what we named him. Between Shannon and Doug, we had an absolute blast! There were some long hours as we drove to places, but the two of them provided us with hours of entertainment. Doug always had a camera in our faces asking us funny questions, filming our surroundings, or getting lost. Every time we got back on the bus, we asked, "Where's Doug the Bug?" because he'd be 100 yards away filming something fascinating. Getting back to that seven-hour drive, what stands out most to me were two things, the beauty of the fields we passed bright with yellow mustard seed flowers and the thousands and thousands and thousands of people we drove past that were living on the side of the road. As we drove miles and miles. I saw every kind of makeshift structure imaginable from a sheet tied to some sticks to cardboard and corrugated metal and just blankets or cardboard on the ground. The sheer numbers were overwhelming. How could we ever help this many people? Thankfully before leaving on our trip we talked a lot about the Starfish Thrower. Originally written by Loren Eiseley, it has been adapted to poems and children's stories, and our friend Bob Hopkins had given us a copy of this version:

Once upon a time, there was a wise man who used to go to the ocean to do his writing. He had a habit of walking on the beach before he began his work. One day, as he was walking along the shore, he looked down the beach and saw a human figure moving like a dancer. He smiled to himself at the thought of someone who would dance to the day, and so, he walked faster to catch up. As he got closer, he noticed that the figure was that of a young man and that what he was doing was not dancing at all. The young man was reaching down to the shore, picking up small objects, and throwing them into the ocean. He came closer still and called out, "Good morning! May I ask what it is that you are doing?" The young man paused, looked up, and replied, "Throwing starfish into the ocean." "I must ask, then, why are you throwing starfish in the ocean?" asked the somewhat startled wise man. To this, the young man replied, "The sun is up and the tide is going out. If I don't throw them in, they'll die." Upon hearing this, the wise man commented, **"But, young man, do you not realize that there are miles and miles of beach and there are starfish all along every mile? You can't possibly make a difference!"** At this, the young man bent down, picked up yet another starfish, and threw it into the ocean. As it met the water, he said, **"It made a difference for that one."**

It kept us focused on helping one person at a time. If we helped one person and then they helped one person and if that kept going, pretty soon a whole community could be transformed.

The first school we visited near Lucknow made a huge impression on us. So much so that we still talk about that school and about the reception we received. Despite our Indian LWI representative Kumar's explanation prior to arrival, we were unprepared for all the commotion. There were drummers drumming and children cheering. There were marigold necklaces and a *huge* party as we were escorted into an unlit concrete building with crude wooden desks inside. We were told it was a school but it sure didn't seem like it. There were no lights, just a few window openings with sunlight providing the interior lighting. Behind the school, was a huge dirt courtyard with a few desks and hundreds of children seated on the ground. Trinity found the hand pump first and started drawing water. That would kind of become her trademark action for years to come. We walked over together to see that this was a project my grandparents had funded and the well plaque bore a thank-you and their names. It was immediately emotional for them, and of course, they and my mom cried. We were seeing our efforts and my grandparents' generosity in person and meeting more than 700 children benefiting from a clean water source they could drink from all day.

The entire school and some of the parents had gathered with the youngest children sitting on the ground upfront. Kumar introduced us and the principal and the headteacher spoke and then asked children to come to the front and recite highlights of what they were learning in school. It kind of reminded me of what we did at Providence on Grandparents and Fine Arts Days. A couple of children stood and told stories of how their siblings had died from water-borne diseases. One girl mentioned how this was her first year going to school. **She could now bring water home after school from the hand pump that Paper for Water had funded and meet her family's need for clean water each day.**

While there was a lot of food that looked tasty, Kumar had cautioned us about eating. He said that obviously everyone wanted to be generous to the guests, but it wouldn't be a good idea if we ate any food that at home would require refrigeration. We carefully selected a few items that we hoped wouldn't be too spicy, and all the children and teachers ate, and everyone looked happy as we celebrated. Next, we sat in a classroom with the older students so we could teach them how to fold origami. We were powerfully affected by the stark difference between our classrooms at home and the one we were sitting in now. The floors were dirt and the walls were made of an open brick pattern to let in light. The desks, only supplied for older students, were a rough piece of wood without drawers and instead of a chair, the students sat on wooden benches, and yet over 700 children were receiving an education. We visited several more schools and had a similar experience at each one. No electricity, no computers, no fancy buildings or amenities. This generated *a lot* of discussion with our parents as to how it was possible for children to be getting an education with so little, while our country

She could now bring water home after school from the hand pump that Paper for Water had funded and meet her family's need for clean water each day.

spent so much on schools, buildings, and everything else and didn't seem to be doing a better job educating our students. The push for so much more spending at home seemed out of place when millions of children here needed a bathroom or a clean drink of water.

After a couple of long days of school visits, we felt exhausted but filled with joy. We had learned and experienced so much and met thousands of school children now drinking clean water. The kids loved learning to fold origami and we were grateful to be able to teach something to the students since we felt like we were learning far more from them. Every day we'd get behind schedule and on our last day of school visits, we were running extra late. This meant that we'd need to make part of the long drive to Varanasi in the dark. That might not seem like a big deal to you if you are reading this book from a location in the world with well-paved and well-lit roads. But driving in India is a whole other experience. How do you describe driving on rural roads in this area of India? Well, to start with there is a lot of praying! Every day we had driven, we had seen every animal imaginable share the road with us, from camels to stray farm animals and dogs. We learned that cows had the right of way and had seen people drive into oncoming traffic on the highways rather than wait for an exit to turn around. It was pitch dark that night as our driver navigated large pots holes and animals on the roads. We were relieved and grateful when we arrived safely in Varanasi, a huge city that has existed for over 3,000 years.

We visited with Kumar, his biological family, and all his adopted children. While he and his wife were of Indian descent, they had both been raised and educated in Canada and had come back to live in India as adults. Some of these children had been left on the streets in wooden crates and boxes and now had a beautiful home, a family that loved them, and an education. I had so much fun playing with all the children living in their compound. We were struck by the fact that the kids all shared a big bunk room. One room for boys and one for the girls. Each child had only *one* dresser drawer for all their clothing. We wondered how many of our friends at home could fit everything they had into only one drawer. We knew that we certainly couldn't. We had so much. That night, we walked down to the Ganges and learned about the Hindu tradition of cremating the dead. According to Hindus, the Ganges is a sacred river that descended from heaven to earth. There is no better place for a Hindu to die and be cremated as they believe they will skip the reincarnation cycle and go directly to Nirvana.

Our last project visit wasn't one funded by Paper for Water but symbolized everything we were trying to accomplish. As we drove several hours into the countryside, the paved roads became sand and the sprawling city completely disappeared. Our destination was a high school and junior college for girls that wasn't close to any town but situated in the middle of several rural communities. Students biked and walked long distances to get to school. Before this school was built, the girls in the area did not have the opportunity to study and most would be married by the age of 16. Being a remote location, a water project and latrines made it possible to build the school. These girls were now receiving an education rather than an early marriage proposal. The result was a complete transformation of the nearby communities. We loved meeting these students and were inspired by the impact that a simple water project had made. We were fired up to go home and raise a lot more money to help a lot more people. After celebrating the New Year in Jaipur and my dad's birthday we returned to Delhi, where we visited paper sellers at the market, selecting absolutely gorgeous cotton rag paper. One store, in particular, seemed to have more tempting patterns and paper than we could possibly carry home. Thank you to some of our friends who have gone back to this specific store in the Delhi market to resupply us.

We asked questions and learned that Kohler had not engaged with the community in advance to provide health and sanitation education prior to doing the installation. We are not criticizing here because we know that everyone's heart was in the right place and charitable work often has a learning curve. One of the reasons that we like partnering with LWI is because they are great about preparing the community before a well is dug or a sanitation project is installed. They only work with communities who reach out to them asking for help. This list is **long** *and sometimes years go by before funding is available. This motivates us to raise as much money as we can to help shorten the waiting period. Prior to project implementation, there are typically six months of sanitation training and community planning. Together they create a program to repair, maintain and protect their project so it will serve their needs into the future. They make sure that latrines are built and that open defecation is eradicated to protect the purity of the water source. Then they stay connected to the community for up to two years after the well is placed. They*

> *make sure all community members have access to the water, that someone is trained appropriately to make repairs if the pump breaks and that life-saving sanitation practices are being followed. These long-term investments are key to the success of the new system. I like that the members of the community ask for the well. it's not just an outsider saying you need this. This promotes community buy-in. Not to mention, it respects their dignity. Often there is a nominal charge for each member, or the community employs someone to staff a water kiosk where water can be sold. These funds give the community revenue needed to make well repairs into the future.*

While in India, we visited the headquarters of Kohler and learned about their efforts to help with health and sanitation. They told us how they'd tried putting a latrine, toilet, and sink in a community, but shortly after the installation, everything was stolen and vandalized. It got me thinking, *Why would someone vandalize something so beneficial?*

Our most interesting official trip in Delhi was to visit the US Ambassador to India, Nancy Powell, and her Deputy Secretary Kathryn Stevens. When Dad had purchased our tickets to India back in October, he reached out to Ambassador Powell because he had learned that prior to becoming an ambassador she had been a schoolteacher. He thought it would be great if we met her and told her about our project in India to bring clean water to communities so that little girls like us could go to school. He sent a letter requesting a meeting before we went to India and then waited a month.

When he hadn't heard back, he sent an email and waited another two weeks with no response before sending yet another email. Undeterred, he then sent an email to a friend of ours whose sister was Deputy Director Kathryn Stevens. At the same time, he asked me to send Ambassador Powell an email and say that I was nine years old and that I'd like to meet with her while I was visiting India. Within a day, I received a response saying that she'd be in Delhi during the holidays, and we could meet with her any time that was convenient for us. Two days later, Dad got an email from Deputy Director Stevens saying that she was excited to help us put the meeting together.

So the day after we arrived in India, I climbed in a van with my family and headed toward the US Embassy, about 30 minutes away from our hotel. After about an hour, we realized that our driver was lost and didn't know where he was going. We couldn't communicate with him, and it took us a while to locate someone on our phone that could speak to him and give him directions. The upside was that we got to see a lot of the city of Delhi, from wealthy neighborhoods to slums.

When we finally showed up at the US Embassy, we were two hours late! It took us an additional 30 minutes to go through security. Since we had to leave our phones and cameras at the guardhouse, we have no photo documentation that this meeting ever occurred but when we were finally led to Ambassador Powell's office, she was so gracious. Even though we were ridiculously late, she cleared out her schedule and met with Katherine and me for over an hour. She took us on a tour of the embassy, which is architecturally a scaled-down version of the Kennedy Center in Washington, DC. She talked to us like we were adults and made us feel so welcome. I'll remember that meeting as long as I live. She was so empowering and encouraging. I'm pretty sure that whatever my dad thought would be accomplished by meeting her was more than achieved.

On the van ride back to the hotel, Dad gave us a teaching moment and said, "Isabelle, you know that I'm a doctor and the CEO of a small company. I actually pay Ambassador Powell's salary through the taxes I pay the US government. Did you notice that she didn't respond to me? *But* she responded very quickly to you. And do you know why? It's because you are a child doing adult work and that is inspirational to people. You're nine. You've got a window of opportunity here until you're an adult and people will treat you the way they treat me. You've got to capitalize on this short period of time and make the most of it. You and your sisters can help so many people."

Now that I'm 18, I can already see the ways people treat me differently than when I was younger. I want to convince more people that children can make a difference and that we should listen to them more, embrace their view that all things are possible and not tamp down their enthusiasm with adult realities.

When leaving India, our flight was delayed by smog and we narrowly made it out before the New Delhi airport grounded flights for three days. Headed back to the US, I felt rejuvenated and excited about raising more money for more water projects around the world. I had seen firsthand that Katherine and I were making a fundamental change in people's lives. We were literally changing the course of people's destinies, not just simply allowing more children to survive infancy but changing their life opportunities from marrying someone at age 14 to getting an education that could lift them out of cyclical poverty. Even at nine, I fully grasped how profound this was. It wasn't just motivating, it was galvanizing. We needed to raise more money!

Epilogue from India: After we left Shannon in the Varanasi airport, she had hopped a train to Agra (which is a story that she'll have to tell when she writes her memoirs.) While there, she met up with her boyfriend, and as they were touring the Taj Mahal, he dropped to one knee, whipped out an engagement ring, and proposed! She would soon become Shannon Escarra, and we were honored to be invited to her wedding.

2014
AND THE COMMUNITY GROWS

"Alone, we can do so little. Together, we can do so much."
Helen Keller

Earth Day

Isabelle

Our first time to participate with volunteers at Earth Day Texas was in 2014. The reason we got involved was the Crow Museum and Trammell Crow Jr., the philanthropist and businessman who started what is now known as EarthX. Since it began, hundreds of thousands of people visit Fair Park every year for the event. He's the reason the event has evolved into the amazing production that it is today. Because we knew him through the Crow Museum, we received an invitation to participate in the day's festivities. In addition to a **Paper for Water** booth in the exhibit hall, the organizers gave us a stage and asked us to present for four hours straight. I helped write a 15-minute presentation with our volunteers and planned to take turns delivering it over and over with a fifteen-minute break in between. My favorite part of the presentation was bringing someone up on stage, where I'd instruct them to carry a jerry-can water jug across the stage and give facts about children carrying a similar jug. Most people had never carried a 40-pound jerry can of water and many struggled to pick it up. We wanted people to experience what millions of children were forced to do by thirst every single day. We also included information on water conservation and sustainability.

It was really a lot of fun, but Katherine and I were grateful we didn't need to do the whole thing by ourselves. Our dedicated volunteers who were the same age as us made the load lighter since we divided the presentations and three of us would present while two of us could take a break. The five of us gave our little presentation multiple times sharing our mission with hundreds of new people.

• • •

Caring Institute Dinner

Isabelle

I think I've probably mentioned this, but Dad's a doctor. He had the extreme good fortune of hiring my first-grade teacher as his executive assistant. Mrs. Thornhill easily makes the top five list of my all-time favorite teachers, and when Dad learned that she was looking for a job, he reached out to her and said that he would circulate her resume. After he looked at it, he didn't circulate it to anyone because he realized that (1) she was way overqualified to be teaching first grade with an MBA from SMU, and (2) she was way overqualified to be his executive assistant. But if he hired her, it'd be a win-win. She wanted some flexibility in her schedule and said that she wanted to help with tutoring my sister and me if the opportunity arose.

Mrs. Thornhill was a huge help in the early years of **Paper for Water** and has been a constant supporter. In her spare time at work, she would search for Youth Leadership Awards and Scholarships. When she found appropriate ones, she filled out the applications and coordinated recommendation letters or wrote them herself. It was through her research that we were recognized by the Caring Institute in 2014 and inducted into the Caring Institute Hall of Fame.

The Caring Institute was started by an amazing gentleman named Val Halamandaris. Mr. Halamandaris founded the National Association of Home Care and Hospice, and in 1985, after meeting Mother Teresa, he created the Caring Institute, which is now located in Washington, DC, in the restored home of Frederick Douglass, the abolitionist, and civil rights leader. Mr. Halamandaris loved to tell everyone that Mother Teresa looked him in the eye and charged him with doing something to encourage Americans to do more for others. She said that the poverty of spirit was far greater in the USA than the physical poverty in India. Of course, you can't exactly say no to Mother Teresa and so the Caring Institute came to be.

Since the awards dinner was in Arizona, we flew to Phoenix for the celebration. I remember it being a late night for us, and not only that, but we were also a little jet-lagged and not on Arizona time. (Or maybe that's me trying to give Katherine a pass for later.) After we checked into this really nice hotel, we hopped into a shuttle van that carried us to the awards dinner. Every year, the Caring Institute has a huge gala, and for the year we were recognized, it was in Scottsdale at a fancy resort.

At the mixer, I didn't know any of these people, but Dad pointed out Jane Seymour and pulled out his phone, and googled some of the movies that she'd acted in, in case we got to talk to her. Katherine and I got our pictures taken with Representative Gabby Giffords and her husband Mark Kelly, who was an astronaut but not yet a US senator. We spent a good deal of time talking with the US Surgeon General, Regina Benjamin, who was a pediatrician and knew how to talk to kids.

The pre-party was in a beautiful outdoor garden, and if I'd known that beforehand, I might not have chosen that evening as the first time to wear high heels. The heel of my shoe kept digging into the grass, building my annoyance with each step. I'm pretty great at walking in heels now, but at the time I kept stumbling and tripping over my own feet. Looking back on it is way more humorous than it was then!

Pictures and drinks took well over 90 minutes. By the time we went into the ballroom for dinner, it was 8:30 p.m., which was 10:30 p.m. Dallas time. I was really excited because alongside Representative Giffords, her husband, and Jane Seymour, two of the other winners of the Caring Institute Award were President Bill Clinton and the World Champion boxer, Muhammed Ali. They hadn't been at the picture session, but I was still holding out hope that they might be at the awards ceremony and I could shake their hands and talk to them after the event was over. I'll be honest, I really wanted to meet President Clinton's wife, Hillary, and find out what it was like to have been a senator and secretary of state. Knowing how much I loved traveling, I wondered if she loved it as much as I did.

Well, big disappointment, no Clintons and no Muhammad Ali. To top the disappointment off was the concern that my co-CEO, who was supposed to be delivering a speech with me on stage, was sound asleep. While I was super fascinated and interested in listening to all of these amazing people tell their stories and receive their awards, she, on the other hand, had fallen asleep and had lain down next to Trinity underneath our table. Her shoes had fallen off. So there she was, barefoot and passed out at the awards dinner. In all honesty, I think I'd taken my shoes off too, but at least I was still conscious! Now, I see it as a funny moment, but then, I was a little embarrassed like, oh my goodness, what is she doing and why is she doing this?

By 11 p.m., we still hadn't been awarded our plaque or delivered our speech. With Katherine still asleep, I kicked her, and she insisted that she was listening with her eyes closed. Although Dad looked a little concerned about the direction this was headed, he nudged me and whispered, "Let her sleep for 10 or 15 minutes."

The other speakers droned on and on and on.

11:15…11:30.

Finally, it looked like they might be moving on to recognizing the young adults. Dad reached down and tried to shake Katherine. Nothing happened. Her body just rolled with his shakes. She was passed out cold and there was no reviving her! I got down on the ground and started shaking her under the table. Softly, she mumbled, "Stop it."

Dad reached down, picked her up gently, put her head on his shoulder, and walked out of the dining hall into a courtyard where he was able to get her to open her eyes. By this point, I was *freaked out*! We were going on stage in less than fifteen minutes and my co-CEO not only didn't know where she was but couldn't remember any of her lines. Dad got her a quick glass of ice water and peeked into the dining hall to see that the first kid being recognized was up on stage giving his speech.

Katherine finally woke up a bit and realized that she had her fancy dress on and wasn't at home in bed. With only five minutes until we went on stage, she finally started working with me and remembering her lines.

Just before midnight, we delivered our speech, the last speech of the evening. We received a standing ovation, but I'm unclear if it was because our speech was so awesome or because everyone was ecstatic that ours was the last one!

· · ·

Ghost Ranch Community Camp

Katherine

Every summer for as long as I can remember, my family and I have gone out for two weeks to a Presbyterian camp in New Mexico called Ghost Ranch. It has become well known for being where Georgia O'Keeffe spent her summers. It's absolutely gorgeous there and something I look forward to all year. The second week of our stay is always Community Camp week. This is a week when local kids come out to the ranch and do lots of outdoor activities and art projects. In the past years, we have been a part of the program and folded with the kids.

One year, in particular, stands out to me. We had been trying to figure out what to fold and decided on one of our most used folds, the star, or more accurately the Bascetta star. (Thank you Paolo Basscetta for letting us use your amazing design to change so many lives!) Before we started the actual folding, we passed out markers and told the kids to write some of their strengths and skills. I remember some of them writing things like soccer, eating chips, and drawing. We then let them cover the page in doodles and whatever else they felt like writing.

Next, we taught them how to fold their pieces. Afterward, my dad explained to them how each piece represented their talents and gifts. Then, we proceeded to assemble them all into one massive star.
He took a book off one of the shelves and placed it on top of the star. A little girl actually took a panicked step toward the star thinking it would be crushed under the weight. However, the star was completely unfazed.

My dad explained how a single folded piece could never support the weight of a book, but when they were all combined, they could. He compared this to a community and how they could accomplish much more when people combined their gifts. However, when you remove even one of the many pieces, the structural integrity disappears and the star collapses under the weight of the book. Similarly in a community, you may think your talents are unimportant but the truth is that your unique talents are what give a community structural integrity.

2015
OUR WORK EXPANDS

*"Let us not become weary in doing good,
for at the proper time we will reap a harvest
if we do not give up."*
Galatians 6:9

One Year Road Trip

Isabelle

The One Year Road Trip was a multimedia film project started by the Webb family of five. Not only did they want to do something super awesome and adventurous, but they also wanted to expose their three kids to other kids making a difference in all 50 states. They set out to showcase kids' stories and inspire others to do their part to change the world. In every state, they would meet and interview at least two kids who were trying to change the world by doing something awesome. They took a whole year off, mapped a road trip to all 50 states, and planned to track their journey in real-time. Across the country, they interviewed projects started by kids like us which included all sorts of organizations, everything from helping at homeless shelters, food pantries, and collecting clothes and shoes for kids. Then they compiled cute little episodes from the interviews. The kids, who were about our age, were the ones who filmed and edited, which of course we loved.

In March of 2015, the Webb family came to Dallas and wanted to interview us! We invited them to help at one of the Crow Collection family days and film us while we were in action. While Katherine and I were interacting with people, the Webb family set up a time-lapse camera of our table to capture everyone coming and going. For some reason, I thought that was the coolest thing. They filmed people coming to learn how to fold, and they also visited our home and captured what I thought then to be a crazy number of ornaments in our house. Retrospectively, I think it was hardly anything. While at our house, Katherine and I did some sit-down interviews with the kids, a fun change of pace for us because we were used to being interviewed by adults.

When I saw the final video about our project, I was impressed and thought it was pretty unique and well crafted. We actually used it in our presentations for years. The Webb family and their One Year Road Trip project helped us realize that we weren't alone and that there are so many other kids like us who are doing inspiring projects. The fact that the Webb children were the stars made it so much more interesting. One of the things that I've seen over and over again is that there are a lot of kids doing awesome stuff. This experience proved that.

The adventure wheels in our brains started turning and wondering, *How could we take **Paper for Water** on the road?* I'd say they definitely gave us a little inspiration because not too long after interacting with them, our family began to plan a trip around the world!

One Year Road Trip

• • •

The Honor Flight

Isabelle

So remember the Caring Institute Awards Dinner in Arizona?

Before the event, we'd debated whether or not to miss school and fly out to Phoenix. We went to the awards dinner not really knowing what to expect, but when we got there, we were blown away by the people attending. One of the honorees, Jeff Miller, started and ran an amazing program called Honor Flight that touched my heart. They flew veterans from all over the country to DC to visit their war memorial, especially WWII vets.

> *Being involved in philanthropy has shown me how goodness spreads out to the people around you, and even across generations because in April of 2015, the Honor Flight guys coordinated with my family to have my great-grandfather, James Hanifen, participate in the program.*

When he exited the plane with the other men, there was an entire welcoming committee. People cheered and waved American flags while a band played. Balloons and handmade signs waved in the air as a water cannon salute went off. It was such a cool way to bless his service. I felt grateful to be the connection that led to this honor for my great-grandfather, who'd never visited the World War II memorial and share the experience with him.

During our time in DC, we also toured the Caring Institute headquarters. Mr. Halamandaris showed us our picture hanging on the wall and took us on a tour of Frederick Douglass's house. It is no coincidence that Mr. Halamandaris bought Frederick Douglass' house as the headquarters for the Caring Institute. Mr. Douglass was a phenomenal man committed to changing and inspiring the United

States to be more than it was during the Civil War. We had a wonderful visit with Mr. Halamandaris as he shared stories about different people who had won the award in the past. Famous winners included the Dalai Lama, Muhammed Ali, Bill Clinton, Jane Seymour, and many senators. There were regular people like us on the wall too, all of us trying to make the world a better place.

It was inspiring and humbling to see our names and photo with theirs and to discover more of the work that people are doing in this world to make other people's lives better. I'm sad to say that Mr. Halamandaris passed away in 2017, but I know that I am so lucky to have met him and been inspired by him to continue to do the work we do.

• • •

A Little Adds Up to a Lot

Katherine

Living in the United States it's hard not to think that things have to be perfect or started on a really big scale. My Aunt Ellen always tells us, "Go big or go home." And while we do want to dream big and achieve our fullest potential, we have also witnessed the truth that sometimes the smallest things make the biggest impact. I think that everyone assumes that our favorite donors are always the biggest ones and it is true that those gifts have the power to transform an entire community. Donations don't just make our mission possible, they inspire us to keep going. In the summer of 2015, we met Erik at an employee meeting at Hawaiian Falls, a local Dallas waterpark, where we were given an opportunity to tell everyone about Paper for Water. Erik was a golf cart driver that ferried guests back and forth to the parking lots. Each day he'd garner a few dollars in passenger tips, often in coins that slowly added up. Erik listened to our presentation and was so moved that he approached us afterward and gave us every single tip he had been given so far that summer. Not ten percent, not twenty percent, he gave 100 percent. We were blown away. We were deeply moved and forever impacted. All of a sudden the story of the widow's mite came home.

This was truly a gift of the heart because Erik had a heart for others. We still talk about Erik and his generosity. At the end of the summer, he invited us and our most dedicated youth volunteers to come for a day of free swimming and fun and as many sodas as we wanted to drink. He also gave us the rest of his tips from the summer. Erik's example showed us that we could indeed do and give so much more. A gift given from the heart is never small and I like to tell people that "when you give a lot, you get a lot and sometimes you get more than you gave."

First Trip to Smith Lake

Katherine

DigDeep is an incredible organization on a mission to bring running water to Americans. Yes, Americans. It surprises a lot of people to find out that there are people in the United States who have no running water. I know it did me. eighty percent of the over two million people in the US without running water live on native American Reservations and DigDeep, though based in California, has identified hundreds of communities in the US in need of clean running water. One of our favorite board members, Tricia Bridges, called one day and excitedly said she'd just heard a story about DigDeep on NPR and that we needed to help. So we called George McGraw, director and founder of DigDeep, and that led to a wonderful and meaningful friendship that has impacted us in countless ways.

As a family, we go every summer to a ranch in New Mexico, which happens to be less than 200 miles away from one of DigDeep's larger projects. We asked George if we could meet his team and visit the Navajo community of Smith Lake. I didn't know then that we'd also be visiting what would become our longest water project fundraiser ever. We fell in love with the people we met, the beautiful place where they lived, and the local mission, St. Bonaventure, which served the community in countless ways. The biggest treat was meeting Darlene, fondly known as the water angel. Darlene was a school bus driver, but between morning pick-ups and afternoon drop-offs she served as a water lifeline to her community for hundreds of miles around. Every day she drove a food-grade water truck to deliver water as far as 50 miles to families in need.

She is the eyes and ears of hundreds of community members and has dedicated her life to serving others. She actually drove us around in her water truck and introduced us to people on the reservation. Two hundred fifty homes without running water had been identified for an ambitious plan to bring a home water system to them rather than continue to fill large barrels with water outside the homes. Many of these houses did not have electricity. And without running water they didn't have indoor sinks, toilets, or showers! It was hard for me to imagine living without what I had considered necessities and was now seeing as luxuries. How can you do well in school if you're worried about how you smell because you haven't showered in two days? How can you hold down a full-time job if you have to drive 40 miles to a friend's house to shower before work? How can you stay healthy if you can't wash your hands at home or boil water to make food at home? And what if you don't have a car?

> *While visiting a home, a little girl showed us to an outhouse and said, "That's where we use the restroom." A woman showed us the tank of water that was supposed to last her family of six for a month. Another man washed his face and hair from a bucket in his living room.*
>
> *I discovered that some people had a water well, but because of uranium mining on their land in the 1950s, the water was contaminated. People with cars were driving long distances to get water, or if they didn't have a car, they walked or hoped for a delivery from Darlene. The fact that they couldn't use the water that was right beneath their feet was crazy and mind-blowing. After this visit with George and Darlene, we got super fired up about helping the community.*

I was sad when I found out that over two million people don't have clean water in the United States and I wanted to help them. I had known poverty existed and I'd seen it, but I was blown away by what I saw, by the kind of poverty people were living in here in the United States. To be completely honest, I was angry. I mean, *they were living in America and didn't have access to the bare necessities!?* It seemed like they'd been forgotten. Flint, Michigan, got a lot of media attention when they didn't have safe drinking water, but there have been people without water on reservations for decades.

I didn't understand anything from the government's standpoint, but I felt if someone was living in this country, they deserved access to water.

So you could say this visit motivated us to get the ball rolling and was the precursor to a lot of new fundraising efforts. At the time, I don't think our goal was to help all 250 homes. I think we just wanted to help as many as we could. Later, as we began to help more and more people, eventually the goal became to help the whole community.

• • •

Paper Discovery Center

Isabelle

In 2015, after we had visited Smith Lake, we traveled to Neenah, Wisconsin, for a special family gathering and to visit our very first exhibit at a museum, the Paper Discovery Center. Interestingly enough, Neenah means "water" or "running water" in a local Native American language. Kimberly-Clark, whose brands include Cottonelle, Kotex, Scott, and Kleenex to name a few, was also founded there. There are a lot of paper factories in Neenah, and we actually have some ties to the paper industry there as my great, great step-grandfather, Havilah Babcock, was one of the founders of Kimberly-Clark. We were in neighboring Appleton for the induction of Havilah Babcock into the Paper Hall of Fame, which happens to also be housed in the same museum.

While at our family reunion the prior summer we visited the Paper Discovery Center, which is a very kid-friendly museum about all things paper. We learned how industrial paper is made and how the paper industry has affected Neenah. We even had a chance to make paper ourselves! The museum also featured lots of interactive exhibits and I absolutely fell in love with the place and wanted to try and partner with them. We began brainstorming and talking with key museum employee Sharon Clothier about doing an exhibit that would feature origami and the Paper for Water story. She absolutely fell in love with **Paper for Water** and wanted to make sure this partnership could happen. We came up with the idea for an origami exhibition that would feature the work of some of our dedicated and talented volunteers, and once we pitched the idea to Sharon, she wrote a grant to get funding for the project.

Later, as we began to help more and more people, eventually the goal became to help the whole community.

Our friends at Clampitt Paper Company in Dallas asked for some beautiful paper donations from Neenah and then handed the paper off to our volunteers. I pretty much told them to make whatever they wanted as long as it was really neat. And given that many of our volunteers were seriously talented, I had no worries that the pieces that came back would be worthy of an art exhibit.

If I must say so myself, Sharon and our volunteers did an incredible job and everything looked great. Some ornaments hung in a window display while others were enclosed in large glass cases. As you walked through the exhibit, signs provided information about the history of origami and how it is used today. They also included information on the water crisis and what we are doing to help. One of my favorite parts of the whole exhibit was the fact that as you walked through, the ornaments started out brown, like dirty water, but as you progressed, they gradually became the bright blue of clean water. In the end, everyone had a chance to fold origami, and Tomoko Fuse, one of the most famous origami artists ever even permitted us to use her diagrams to teach one of her designs! Someday I hope we can meet her in person to thank her.

In addition to the many ways that Sharon helped, she set up a meeting to introduce us to one of Kimberly-Clark's board members, Peter Allen, and he brought Edna Guerra along from Kleenex's marketing department. Kleenex had recently started a marketing campaign in which meaningful projects and events around the country were highlighted in hopes of bringing people to tears and they would need to reach for a Kleenex. During our meeting with Mrs. Guerra, we discussed the idea of doing a video with **Paper for Water** that ended up becoming the second most-watched Kleenex video with over five million views, but you will have to keep reading to see how that happened.

• • •

Nickelodeon Filming

Katherine

Now, I know it sounds a little different, but Isabelle and I didn't grow up with television. Our parents aren't anti-technology, but they are very pro-present. Growing up without a lot of technology has had a huge impact on us. I hate to admit that they're right, but TV is a huge time suck. If we would have had it as kids, that's where we would have spent our Saturday and Sunday mornings, which was the time spent on **Paper for Water** activities. I feel like this is important to mention because I think people don't realize how the hours add up over time. I'm not saying watching TV is bad. I have Netflix and I love it, but at a certain point, you have to decide what you value and want to get out of life.

I think my parents were on top of their game raising us because as far as my generation goes, I'll go to a group hangout to be with friends and people will just be on their phones, not being present or really engaging in a conversation. I think it's kinda sad. It's important to be able to connect in real life with people, socially and emotionally. To this day, I have a flip phone and Isabelle didn't get a real phone until the end of her sophomore year. It benefited us both because phones are often used as a social crutch. When a conversation lulls, someone says something awkward, or there's not anything to add, people will just pull out their phone and scroll. Or if in a public space, people will pull out their phones just to have something to do. When you don't have that, you're much more apt to engage with people in conversations. Not having a phone helped with our imagination and creativity, and it definitely helped us be more communicative. This in turn has helped us interact with donors, work with volunteers, and just talk to people in general.

With that being said, for the most part, Isabelle and I *are* rule followers, but everyone knows that kids get away with a little more with their grandparents, right? And while not having a lot of technology has benefited us in so many ways, periodically while at our grandparents' house, we'd binge-watch all the TV shows our friends were always talking about. The rule was that we couldn't get up before six, but from six until they got up, we watched TV. That's all the TV time I got, and that's all I really needed. So, when Nickelodeon contacted us about filming a segment for their *Halo Effect* series, I knew it was a big deal. Hey, I had watched enough to at least keep me relevant!

The whole filming process was incredibly fun and exhausting! Having a film crew follow you around is so neat. We'd never heard of Craft Services, but that turned out to be our favorite part of filming. For the entire two weeks of filming, Craft Services' sole job was to keep us fed and make our lives better. First and foremost they made sure that we had all the right kind of food and snacks we wanted. They took my little sister to ballet. They drove us around and ran any errand that we needed. It was awesome!

The shoot days were lengthy, often twelve hours long, but the whole crew made it fun. Isabelle and I can be professional for a very long time, but I remember one day being so long that we kind of hit a cracking point and started laughing at everything. Isabelle and I went into the bathroom at one of the gift fairs. We were mic'd up and didn't really think about it. Everything we'd say to each other and to other people, the camera crew could all hear. So sometimes we'd just talk to them in our little mic, "Hey, what's a girl gotta do for a Rice Krispie treat around here?"

While the messaging was accurate, we staged events throughout filming. I know Mom was stressed over the logistics and so glad that we aren't doing this all the time. One day during the shoot, the crew came out to the barn with us to get some footage of us riding horses. Of course, the camera caught me on an off day! I was so frustrated that it seemed like I was not a very good horse rider. I told the producer, "No, y'all, please don't use that." I kept thinking, *Where's my retake on that?*

By that point, I had learned there's not much reality in reality television. For one of the segment's scenes, we calculated a 300-ornament goal with our parents in the living room. I don't think we could've ever made it as child actors. For one thing, our voice pitch kept fluctuating. We'd probably cost production a fortune because it took so many takes to get the shot for the re-enactment of that goal.

In addition to shooting our everyday lives and **Paper for Water** activities in Texas, they traveled with us to New Mexico to visit our project for the Navajo Nation in Smith Lake. We'd set up a folding party for Darlene and several families at the mission office, and I couldn't wait to see the look on Darlene's face when we'd hand her the check for $15,000! First, we gave her the Navajo ornament to unwrap.

"Now, we have one more thing," said Isabelle as she handed her the envelope.

When Darlene opened the envelope, she started crying and we all hugged her. I think that was the most real and unstaged interaction of the whole episode.

Afterward, Isabelle and I played on the playground with the Navajo children. Spinning around on the merry-go-round, I got to have a moment where we were all kids. I wasn't just one of the Adams sisters helping them. It reminded me that everyone is the same and that they were kids just like me. A child is a child. Everyone loves to learn; everyone loves to play, despite where you live or what access to amenities you have. It can be a hard topic to breach, but the moment was a very humanizing interaction.

Sometimes, it's easy to be all high and mighty, like when you are helping someone out and giving them something that they can't do themselves. Sometimes it feels awkward when interacting to give, maybe because of the assumption that they're embarrassed to accept the help or of how I would feel if I were in their position. But I feel like when you actually interact, people are grateful, and you can see how strong and independent they are. They are very capable, self-sufficient, and normal. It's the idea of giving someone a hand up, rather than a handout.

Sometimes during interviews, we get questions like why do you give of your time and efforts to people you don't even know and will probably never meet? Our answer is always multifaceted because there isn't just one reason we do Paper for Water. One of the reasons has always been, "As blessed people, born in the United States with access to all the basic amenities, an education, and so much more, we feel like we are called to bless other people." However, another thing we say all the time is, "By giving a community clean water, you are enabling children to receive an education, gaining the tools they need for success later in life. You really never know what they will grow up to accomplish; they might even one day find the cure to cancer or Alzheimer's and in turn, could end up saving our lives."

After all, you never know what "tornado event" an action like that will help create.

2016
OUR BIG BREAK

"It always seems impossible until it is done."
Nelson Mandela

The Kleenex Video

Isabelle

Remember the Paper Discovery Center installation and the meeting
we had with Edna Guerra from Kleenex? Well, during that meeting we
talked about our recent visit to the Navajo reservation and the poverty
we had witnessed as well as the amazing work that DigDeep was doing
to help improve the lives of those living there. We concluded that it
was the perfect project for Kleenex to film as it would give them the
opportunity to see our work up close and in person rather than try to
organize a trip to a project overseas.

We planned a secret project to help a family over our spring break in
March. Our family drove out to meet up with the film crew and a team
from DigDeep. The video, *The Gift of Water,* centered around a family
who had never had running water in their home. St. Bonaventure had
given them a barrel or two that was supposed to last them for a long
time, but it just wasn't enough. It was heartbreaking to hear the mom
say, "I really want water for my kids. It makes us feel bad because they
want to shower, and we don't have that."

Luckily, we could help change that! To keep the project a surprise, before we'd arrived, the family had been told they were going to Albuquerque to do some volunteer work. They'd stay in a hotel and help out for a few days. While they were out of town, we partnered up with DigDeep and worked to install a water tank, pump, and sink. We didn't have time to put in a shower, but that would happen after they returned.

While **Paper for Water** had helped fund over 100 water projects by this time, we'd never been to a well dig site before because we hadn't been old enough. It was really special to be on-site for the actual installation of this project and get to help out a little bit. Over the course of the three days, as other people worked a backhoe to dig the water tank, Katherine and I helped assemble some of the plumbing for the sink, and we both helped install the sink in their house. A big water truck came to fill up the tank, and the whole time we were there, the film crew was right along with us. We worked long hours for several days to complete everything before the family came back.

I was so excited for the family to come home. The moment they did was really special, to see them experience something for the first time that they'd never had before. Everyone who had participated in the installation lined up, cheering and clapping as their car arrived. We stood with George McGraw of DigDeep as he said to the family, "We planned, over the last couple of days, to get you guys out of the house so that we could build a special surprise for you, and it's inside waiting for you to discover it."

The mom's smile widened as she turned on the sink for the first time, and the dad lifted one of his two daughters to run her hands beneath the sink spout. Wiping away his tears, he said, "It's going to make things a lot easier for us to have running water. Thank you."

Later on, after the surprise reveal, I talked to their two little daughters and played with them. In the past, I'd met people who'd received a water project, like in India, but this was the first time I was able to have a real conversation because there was no language barrier. Chatting with them and seeing when they turned on the tap for the first time made it clear to me the impact that we were having in these people's lives.

Honestly, when I watch the video now, I remember how happy seeing them with running water made me, but it also humbled me. I'd been so fortunate to have access to clean, running water my whole life when there are people just a few hours away that have never had it. I don't think running water is something a lot of kids, or even adults, ever think about in the United States; we all just assume that everyone has it. I can't help but place myself in their shoes. What if Katherine and I had been born in a place that did not have clean water? This is one of the most important stories for us to share I think, because contrary to what most people think, you don't have to go overseas to witness the water crisis; it's right next door.

• • •

Nickelodeon Premiere

Katherine

In June of 2016, we hosted a premiere party for our Nickelodeon episode of *The Halo Effect*. With two weeks of filming crammed into 22 minutes, I was a bit nervous about what exactly the producers would or would not include. Of course, my mind immediately drifted to what might be mortifying! I hadn't watched it yet and would be seeing it for the first time with all of the other people there. The nerves were intensified because a group of my classmates was there to watch it too.

Over the years, I've always felt a bit weird talking about **Paper for Water** with my friends, which shouldn't be the case. Maybe I didn't want them to feel pressured to do something because they were my friends. Whatever the reason, this was one of the events I distinctly remember a lot of my friends attending.

They've always known about **Paper for Water**, and they knew that we ran a nonprofit, but not many of them had ever really gotten involved, which was partially Isabelle's and my fault because of the line we'd drawn between friends and **Paper for Water.**

So I sat with them in the auditorium of the hospital my dad worked in at the time, eating pizza and awaiting my embarrassment. Of course, their response was way better than I'd anticipated! One of my classmates saw himself in it, got really excited, and shouted, "Hey, look! It's the back of my head. I'm right there!"

"Wow, Katherine," another guy friend said, "You actually do stuff!"

"Yeaaaa," I said, laughing it off. I knew he knew I routinely missed school for events, but I'd never told him where I'd been or what I'd done.

One cool thing about the video was that it highlighted some of the volunteers who had been with us for a long time or from the very beginning. Media pieces and TV spots are generally two or three minutes at most and don't have time to highlight the important work of our volunteers. This one was great because it really put the spotlight on a lot of our volunteers who don't get the recognition they deserve. It was awesome to have them in it and for them to get to see themselves talking and folding.

When I re-watched the episode recently, there was a moment when I realized how much time I've spent on this project during my life. In the video, I looked so tiny and young. At one point, we mentioned how we had been doing **Paper for Water** for four years. It seems crazy to think we were only four years into the journey then. So much had happened leading up to that point, but if I only knew then how much more was to come!

Halo Effect Episode

Our Big Break

● ● ●

Isabelle

Remember Karla Buie from a few years ago? Our board member who we met at the Garrett Boone lunch at The Container Store headquarters? Well, toward the end of 2016, we had asked her to help us plan our first annual event and expand our network.

We knew that she was friends with Hedda Dowd, the restaurant owner of *rise no. 1*, a popular favorite in Dallas. She used to be a vendor to Neiman Marcus and knows absolutely everyone in Dallas because of her fantastic restaurant. We asked Karla, "Would you be willing to ask Hedda for a gift certificate for the silent auction?"

"Of course, I'll call her today," Karla offered.

Karla called and told Hedda all about Paper For Water and our request. After listening, Hedda told Karla, "Anyone can give a gift certificate. I want to do something more. We couldn't wait to meet Hedda and find out what she had in mind. She invited Karla and our whole family to lunch at her restaurant. Little did we know that this meeting would lead to so many opportunities and connections that we nicknamed her our Fairy Godmother.

I didn't realize at the time how big of a deal that was because I had never heard of *rise,* but it's a super fancy, well-known place.

For the lunch meeting, we brought a computer to show her a little slide show. After we finished, she said, "Can you do it again? I'd love for you to show my managers and staff."

Right at the end of our second presentation, she said, "Girls, give me one second. I need to go make a phone call."

We didn't really know what was going on, but she went off and we continued talking.

"She's super nice. I bet she's doing something good," I said.

A few minutes later, Hedda came back to the table and said, "I just got you an emcee for your event. Shelly Slater, the TV anchor."

"Thank you!" We'd started planning our first-ever annual event fundraiser and hadn't even thought about needing an MC.

This stunned Katherine and me. *Wow, she just went off for five minutes to make a phone call and now we have an amazing MC!* I don't even think Karla was expecting that.

A week later my mom's cell phone rang and it was Hedda asking if we could join her at the Akola launch party at the original downtown Neiman Marcus store. We are going to talk more about Akola later and it is amazing how so many things tie together throughout our story. "Could you and the girls come with me?" she asked. "I want to introduce the girls to Karen Katz."

My mom wasn't available, so we went to the party with Karla. As soon as we arrived, Hedda came and found us. "Two seconds please, girls. I need to briefly introduce you to Ms. Katz and see if we can set up a meeting."

She led us over to Ms. Katz, and when Hedda introduced us, you could see that Ms. Katz was wondering, *Why are there two small children at this event? What are they doing here?*

"These two girls have an organization and are doing amazing work," said Hedda. "They have really beautiful products that you should see."

I could tell from Ms. Katz's body language that her receptivity had shifted and had started to think we may actually have something kind of interesting going on. She arranged a meeting with us and one of the last things she said was, "Make sure you bring plenty of product for us to see."

Well, we really took that to heart because when we went in for our meeting a week later we brought boxes and boxes of ornaments. The meeting room had a massive conference table, and we covered the whole thing in ornaments.

We connected our PowerPoint presentation and Hedda offered to run the lights to make sure we had the most dramatic lighting possible in the conference room. One of the executives came in, sat down, and said, "I'm here for your presentation. Ms. Katz will be here in a few minutes."

Hedda had counseled us to prepare both a three-minute presentation and a thirty-minute one. She said that Karen was extremely busy and we might not get more than the three-minute opportunity. So when Ms. Katz came in, we nervously asked if she wanted our three-minute or thirty-minute presentation. She smiled and said, "The thirty-minute one." We immediately felt more at ease but still nervous as the room was full of Neiman's top executives.

Twice, one of Ms. Katz's assistants came to the room to let her know she had another meeting, but she stayed and kept talking to us. She stayed much longer than the original 30 minutes. All kinds of ideas and questions were being traded around the table. It was incredible and very reassuring because everyone we presented to commented, "Love your product. Absolutely perfect."

Someone else chimed in, "Yes. This could be a very unique fantasy gift. We would like to talk with our team about that."

This one was great because it really put the spotlight on a lot of our volunteers who don't get the recognition they deserve.

When Ms. Katz finally needed to leave, she said, "We need to bring some more people in to see this." A few more people were gathered from down the corporate office hallways and we gave the whole presentation again.

From that point to the end of the year, we went to the downtown Neiman Marcus store every week after school for a meeting to plan for the following year's fantasy gift and retail ornaments for each store. I think we gave more or less the same presentation each week to the various departments involved—store retail, marketing, public relations, catalog, fantasy gift team, and of course our buyers. We loved everyone on the Neiman Marcus team and had no clue how complicated retail was before this. We covered all kinds of planning logistics too. *What style of ornaments do we need to make? How many do they need us to make for each store? What colors? Where are we going to display them? What should the fantasy gift look like? What are the official holiday catalog Pantone colors?* Yep, that was a new word for us. We loved these meetings and everything we were learning.

Neiman Marcus Fantasy Gifts were first offered over 60 years ago and are luxurious, over-the-top gifts that debut each fall on national television. Fantasy Gifts can run into the millions, so our curated collection of over 400 ornaments to fully decorate a large 16-foot tree looked kind of like a bargain. We were going to be the 2017 High/Low gift. $50,000 for the one-of-a-kind collection or $50 for a single limited edition ornament. Plus thousands of ornaments for the nationwide stores. Our volunteers made all this come together, turning fantasy into reality.

We'd had the support of a few small Dallas boutique retailers that believed in our mission, but we'd never had our ornaments in stores nationwide. This was truly the retail jackpot. There was no store more prestigious or glamorous than Neiman's.

This was our first foray into the world of retail on a large scale, and Katherine and I were lucky to have the best team in the world working with us. Our buyers, Howard Feldman and Kim Hartdner were absolutely phenomenal. Howard came to every meeting and gave us advice on pretty much everything. And Kim was so wonderful, she even helped me years later decide which high school to go to. Hedda attended almost every meeting too and always brought us cookies and chocolate from *rise* since we were always hungry right after school. We ate dozens of Hedda's Biscuits Grandmere, but the chocolate is still my favorite.

Before we left for our trip, we started talking to Brittany Underwood, the founder of Akola. Akola isn't just any jewelry company. They actually work with women in Uganda and here in Dallas to make handmade jewelry and give them a living wage. They set goals and are assigned to savings groups that help them achieve the goals they set. These might be anything from buying a bicycle to building a house. In the case of unforeseen disaster or hardship, they have the ability to secure a loan that wouldn't otherwise be possible. Prior to employment, the Ugandan women had been living below the $1.90 a day poverty line. Almost all of them owned only one dress, meaning that after washing their clothing they'd need to stand naked waiting for it to dry. We are talking about extreme poverty conditions.

Since we knew we were going to be in Uganda, we got to thinking, *We make origami, Akola makes paper beads. Both are paper; there's gotta be something we can do with them.* We were working with a paper company called Caspari for one of the retail ornament styles that would be available nationwide. We dreamed up a crazy plan to have the Akola employees fold the paper for these ornaments. Then we decided that all the money raised from these particular African crafted ornaments would be used to fund water projects in the USA. The idea was that Africa would be helping us rather than the stereotypical other way around. We will talk more about this opportunity later, but I want you to know that these women beamed with pride knowing they were able to help someone else.

Our papa often says, "The thirsty aren't who you think they are, they are right here and they are thirsty to help." Well, it turns out that that holds true around the world. Helping others provides a sense of joy and meaning and working with these women proved that absolutely anyone has access to that.

● ● ●

Isabelle

Leading up to our trip around the world, things were crazy and we had an unforeseen turn of events that left us without an executive director with less than two months to departure. Panicked, we immediately put the word out that we needed to hire someone quickly. We also contemplated closing things down while we were gone. That weekend at dinner with our friends, the Sinasac family, we voiced our fears and concerns. Craig had been traveling a good deal to India for work and had recently visited a water project that he and Anne had funded. It had deeply impacted Craig and he saw clearly what a difference clean water could make. Mom said, "We don't know what to do since we lost our executive director. We are thinking about shutting things down." Immediately Mr. Sinasac said, "You can't because people will die. Bring everything to our house and we will keep things running." That might not sound like a big deal, but our non-profit operation had completely taken over most of the first floor of our house. We stored supplies to make ornaments, supplies for shipping and handling, supplies for doing presentations, our house was full of supplies and of course shelves and boxes full of completed ornaments! This wasn't a casual offer to help, this was a major commitment that came at just the right time. We can never thank Anne and Craig enough for keeping PFW alive while we went on our trip, but we also have to thank their daughters, Emma and Sarah, because they had to deal with PFW invading their house for over 8 months, which I can assure you is no small inconvenience.

The next thing that happened at just the right time was that multiple people we knew suggested the same person as someone to hire to help while we were gone. That's when God put Kayla McCaffrey in our lives. We'd been told by an early mentor, Fred Hoster, that there are a lot of things you teach a person, so start with the heart. Kayla is someone with a heart of gold and is willing to try just about every crazy idea we throw her way. She couldn't actually start working until about a month after we had left the country, so we were a little bit nervous, but board members Scott Conard and Rugger Burke worked closely with Kayla and helped her learn all about Paper for Water.

2017
AROUND THE WORLD

*"The world is a book, and those
who do not travel read only a page."*
Saint Augustine

Peru

Katherine

Doing new things is scary. Traveling to unknown destinations can be frightening. Not knowing what is going to happen because you don't speak the local language is unnerving. Life in general requires a certain amount of trust. Whether it's getting into a cab at night in a foreign country or hopping on a seaplane for the first time and landing on a quickly flowing river, you sometimes have to trust people you've never met.

Through our middle school, Providence, my sisters and I read about brave missionaries and the work they've done around the world. Sometimes those stories ended well, and sometimes the missionary ended up being a martyr. So just because you think you are doing God's work doesn't mean that you'll be safe or that there's no need for caution... or that you won't wake up in the middle of the night in a cold sweat five hours before you're supposed to climb on a small seaplane and leave for a remote part of the Amazon River basin that doesn't have cell service, isn't accessible by car, and would take a boat nine days to get there.

By the time my family got to Peru in January, we had already traveled to Ecuador and the Galapagos. We'd also been to India, Europe, Asia, and Australia on prior trips, so we were not traveling newbs. But this was going to be a different experience. The day before we left for San Lorenzo, we met Jorge, our guide and the CEO of AMA, the implementation partner for Living Water International in Peru. He almost always smiled and was a large man with an easy attitude about him, but he didn't speak English. He spoke Spanish, Quechua, Aymara, and the language of the Kandozi but not English. So we had to have a second interpreter, Rosio. She was so fun, bubbly, and excited to be traveling with us.

Life in general requires a certain amount of trust.

Before we left for Pucallpa with Rosio and Jorge, we connected with Alison Read in Lima. Alison had been our Living Water International representative in Dallas, and it was so great to see her since we'd left the United States almost a month prior. Alison is the neatest person who is always happy. Trinity loves hanging out with her.

In Pucallpa, after checking into our hotel, we all piled into the back of a pickup truck and went for ice cream. What was crazy, and though I didn't truly understand the significance at the moment, we drove past block after block of chainsaw stores. How could so many stores sell chainsaws?! Keep reading because the next day we sadly learned why.

Early the next morning, we were on the road and headed to the SAM Air runway (SAM Air is South American Missions). We arrived a little before 7 a.m., and after weighing our bags and our bodies, we boarded a small seaplane on the lake near the hangar.

We thought we were in the middle of nowhere. I was wrong...we would be shown the middle of nowhere in just a few hours. To say I was nervous is an understatement. I wasn't quite hyperventilating yet. While I wiped the sweat from my hands on my pants, Trinity was making sure that the air sickness bags were in working order. We then backed out off a ramp onto a lake for takeoff. The awesome pilot explained how he would first lift one pontoon off the water to break the adhesive forces of the water and then the second pontoon because the plane didn't have enough lift to break the adhesive forces of two pontoons at the same time. And then we were in the air.

It quickly became obvious why the Amazon is called a rainforest. When we saw huge thunderheads in multiple spots on the horizon, our pilot promptly described how we were going to avoid those. I could tell my dad was super fascinated because he kept asking the pilot questions about doctors getting a pilot license and if there was a need for doctors in the missionary field with their own plane and pilot's license.

Mom, on the other hand, was fixated on the scenery below. Huge swaths of land had been clear-cut, and there were little fires all over the place burning the cut wood. Suddenly, all the things we'd heard in science class about the destruction of the Amazon and how destroying these carbon sinks is leading to climate change were literally happening right below us in real time. All those chainsaw stores in Pucallpa were supplying the destruction of our planet. I think it's difficult for a lot of kids to feel empathy toward a dying rainforest halfway across the world, but suddenly all the statistics gave way to real life. It suddenly came into focus just how serious the issue of deforestation really is, and I think I even saw my mom crying.

There were still swaths of forest that looked untouched and waterways seemed to branch and snake everywhere, but a great deal of the two hours we flew was over complete destruction of what had once been rainforest below. I don't think anything could have prepared us to see what we did. Finally, we landed on a swift-moving river and taxied to the shore. Dozens of curious people came to the shore to see who had arrived.

We hopped in some tuk-tuks and headed to our hotel. Amazingly, everything I saw in the town of San Lorenzo had either been flown in or put on a boat and brought up the Maranon River, a tributary of the Amazon. We checked into our hotel, a concrete building with a corrugated metal roof. Each room had a fan, bed, sink, shower, no hot water, and electricity two hours per day in the morning and two hours at night. Just to clarify the shower was a metal pipe that didn't have enough water pressure to actually wash our hair. So we didn't. It was supposedly the nicest hotel in town. I was very grateful our pilot had told us to keep the earplugs from the plane. I'll explain that later.

We ate all our meals at the same restaurant because they owned a generator. We also ate the same thing for breakfast every morning and then the same meal of chicken and rice every night for dinner. Jorge had hired a boat and driver to take us to the "real" middle of nowhere; every day we'd board this cool, narrow, covered, gas-powered riverboat. The captain brought along his little kids, and Trinity hit it off immediately with the little girl, and for the next few days, they were inseparable. As we knew from previous trips around the world, you can become great friends with someone even when you can't speak their language.

That first afternoon on the boat, the captain pushed down the throttle handle and skimmed over the café latte-colored water. It made me miss my dad's and my morning trip to Starbucks. It also made me realize that we hadn't seen a Starbucks in a month and might not see another one for several more months to come. In less than an hour, the boat slowed, and people came out of the jungle on the water's edge. We pulled up to a dock and exited the boat into a small town. Suddenly, we were surrounded by a huge group of women and children staring at Trinity's blond hair and our white skin. Jorge had told us at lunch that a lot of the people we would meet might not have ever seen a white person before in their lives and that we may be seen as an oddity. It was true! Walking into the community, Trinity very quickly found the **Paper for Water** hand pump and started pumping water and splashing in it.

Everyone was so grateful and friendly, and it was wonderful to engage with people and learn about their communities and their needs.

When we visited several more villages, we learned from the women we met that they needed more hand pumps. Because their village had clean water and kids weren't dying from drinking the dirty river water, more people had moved to their village. Now, it was hard to stand in line to get water every day. They also needed some restrooms because the population in the village was growing so much, and it wasn't safe for the girls to go into the woods to use the restroom. They urgently pleaded with us to help them build more infrastructure in their village. It doesn't end with bringing clean water to a village. Everywhere we went women asked us for bathrooms. Please think about that the next time you are waiting in line for a restroom.

One day as we were leaving the last village and heading home, we had an amazing experience. Our riverboat captain spotted something in the water and quickly pointed us in the direction he saw it. We didn't quite understand what he was talking about, but then we saw a spray of water followed by a pinkish white hump breaking the surface. as the spray dissipated into the air. It disappeared and then another one appeared about 20 feet behind the first one. Rosio started talking to Jorge excitedly and finally told us, "These are pink freshwater dolphins! Jorge has never seen them, and the captain has only seen them a few times in his life."

We learned that it was extremely rare to see these elusive dolphins due to the murky water and their small population. We watched them for about an hour as the captain followed them around the inlet. My dad kept trying to get a good video of them, but they never broke the surface of the water for long periods of time, and it was difficult to tell where they would come up to breathe.

I watched the graceful and beautiful creatures as they broke the inlet's smooth, inky black water and then resubmerged. Watching them mesmerized me. However, I'd later think of them when I learned of the extensive pollution present in the river water. Sadly, the burning Amazon forest was not the only thing suffering from human destruction.

Another reason we went back to the same restaurant every day was that Jorge told us it was the only place he could consistently get food that didn't make him sick. He said it was because the cook understood the need to wash hands and they had a refrigerator that worked and was kept running all the time with a generator. I was suddenly very appreciative of Jorge and his concern about things that in the United States wouldn't have even crossed my mind. I knew not to drink the water or eat uncooked vegetables, but I don't think I would have ever asked the cook if they kept their refrigerator turned on 24/7. After a dinner of chicken and rice, I walked around the block with Allison and met the first of many, many dogs I would have loved to take home. There was one dog I especially loved. Over the next few days, I would slip him pieces of my chicken. I named him Pollo, chicken in Spanish, and desperately pleaded with my parents to let me bring him home with us. It was the first of many, many times my parents told me I was simply not allowed to bring a dog along with us.

After dinner, Jorge said, "We need to go to church."

Seven tribal chiefs from distant villages had walked up to two days to meet the **Paper for Water** girls and Jorge to ask us for help getting clean water. What an interesting experience! We learned from Jorge through Rosio that we were experiencing a break with cultural norms. In the tribal communities along the Amazon basin, tribal chiefs don't acknowledge children, let alone little girls. As a woman elder got up to speak during the evening meeting, Rosio told us, "It is very rare that women are allowed to speak."

Jorge made it clear to us that we couldn't promise anyone that we were bringing them water. Surveys hadn't been done. He didn't know where all these villages were, and there were so many villages ahead of these that had been promised water already. We listened as these village chiefs pleaded with us. It was very evident, despite not speaking their language, what they were asking for.

Jorge spent some time after the event talking to the village chiefs. Afterward, he told us that there were probably some water pumps that we weren't going to visit. He'd confirmed a rumor he had heard about an oil and gas worker who had been killed near one of the villages and concluded that it wasn't safe for us to go near there.

Hot, sweaty, and sticky, we went back to our hotel to get ready for bed. I was excited to hop into the shower. I didn't realize that the lack of electricity meant no hot water. I stood in the shower while a trickle of ice-cold water poured out of the faucet. Desperately trying to wash away the days' worth of sweat and mosquito spray, I continued standing under the trickle until my somewhat irrational fear of malaria from the swarming mosquitoes made me abandon all hopes of getting clean.

Upon exiting the shower, I was met with a wave of warm, humid air and almost immediately began to sweat again. The electricity was on from 8 to 10 p.m. Those two hours were blissful. Isabelle and I laid on the same bed in front of a small fan in an effort to get cool. We decided it would be easier to go to sleep while the fan was still running, but just as we were drifting off, the *discoteca* next door started blasting music. Loud, thumping, bass-heavy music. Then the fan turned off as the two hours of electricity had ended. The following hours were miserable. Our parents had warned us to stay completely covered by the sheet to not get bit by mosquitoes, which resulted in our bed turning into a cocoon of sweat and bug spray. Even though the heat was stifling and the music deafening, I still somehow managed to hear one annoying mosquito buzz around our room for upwards of an hour. Thank goodness we could get some relief with the earplugs from the plane.

The next morning was rainy, hot, and humid. We walked in the rain to breakfast where we had chicken and rice. I was noticing a theme and it was getting a little old. I didn't complain because of what Jorge told me about the refrigerator and the handwashing, but I began to dread the next few days. On the boat, we had some snacks and peanut butter and jelly sandwiches and those were by far the best meals of the week.

It rained so hard that day that the captain could barely see 20 feet in front of him as he navigated the river. We visited two or three villages in the morning and met so many joyful kids and moms who thanked us for bringing them clean water. Even though the villages were muddy and difficult to walk around in with all the standing water, we still had fun. My favorite village had a soccer field outside of its tiny school. The soccer ball was made of plastic bags tied together and the "soccer field" was mostly mud, but I had a blast kicking the ball around with all the kids.

> *One of the villages was different. It didn't have many kids, and none were smiling. We took a picture with them, and they all looked malnourished and sick. Jorge explained that bringing clean water wasn't always the only solution to keeping people healthy. The oil and gas drilling and exploration in the area had introduced toxic chemicals into the river water. There was very little mosquito netting and no screens, so diseases like malaria were still a cause of significant illness in the area. This conversation with Jorge prompted a new project in Mom's head that stuck with her for months, if not years—a hospital riverboat that dispensed screens to all the people along the Amazon. My mom periodically comes up with crazy ideas, and we still tease her to this day about her screen project in the Amazon. That village was a low point for me. It was the hardest one to leave because I knew that the people still needed so much help.*

We spent two more days around San Lorenzo. One day, after traveling three hours down the Maranon, I realized that we were now truly in the middle of nowhere. We hadn't communicated with anyone from home via Facebook or phone or email for three days. If the boat sank in the middle of the wide river or if we were hijacked by river pirates, which we had learned the day before were in fact a real thing, no one would have known where to look for us.

For the last night in San Lorenzo, I was told we were not eating chicken and rice. Instead, we would be treated to fish. I was excited, no, that's definitely an understatement, I was ecstatic! I have never been more excited to eat fish. However, I was not ready for the extreme disappointment that would befall me upon tasting that fish. It was more salt than fish. It was so salty, I wanted to cry. If you've ever accidentally opened your mouth in the ocean, you know how bad it burns. I later learned that the fish had come in on a boat without refrigeration, and the only way they kept it from spoiling was by pouring salt all over it. What a lovely way to end our trip.

Overall, despite the less-than-desirable accommodations and food, our trip down the Amazon was incredible. We learned how the Kandozi honor their dead in little huts outside their main houses by keeping their bodies, sometimes for years. I went fishing in a pouring rainstorm on the Maranon, caught a prehistoric fish, and saw five-year-old boys piloting their own boats on the river. We watched a pod of endangered pink dolphins swimming at sunset. We visited churches and taught origami. And, of course, Trinity made great friends with the cook at our restaurant. The cook even gave Trinity the headdress her daughter had worn when she was a little child. Trinity still has that beautiful, traditional Peruvian costume.

I'd be remiss if I didn't recount the crazy exodus we endured getting back to Lima. On the morning of our departure, SAM Air reported that a huge thunderstorm had rolled in from the Pacific and was between Pucallpa and San Lorenzo. The floatplane would not be coming for us, possibly for days. We decided that we needed to get out of San Lorenzo quickly. With the huge thunderstorm rolling toward us, we could be stuck for days. We raced toward San Lorenzo's tiny airport and grass runway and weighed in. A plane landed and just as we were about to board, an ambulance rolled up with a sick, pregnant woman. Naturally, she was able to jump the line with her family to fly to the hospital. We had to wait for the next plane. Now the funny thing about planes in rural Peru... they take off when they're full, and not on a time schedule. That meant that we'd need to wait for the plane that had just left to fill up in Yurimaguas before it would fly back to San Lorenzo. This process was repeated all day as planes flew a short 40-minute trip back and forth between these two towns. Waiting for a flight to fill could take minutes or it could take hours.

There were no planes from Yurimaguas to Lima, but we could rent a small bus and drive the 80-mile, two-and-a-half-hour drive to Tarapoto, a much larger town with a small airport and flights to Lima the next morning. So that's what we planned to do. As we were taking off from San Lorenzo, I saw the wall of rain and lightning clouds about 70 miles to our west. Oh, and I forgot to mention, our whole group didn't fit on the plane. Alison, Rosio, and Jorge stayed behind to wait for our plane to fill up after it landed and return for them. The storm was moving in, and time was precious!

We landed in Yurimaguas and waited around the airport for a while. Our plane had arrived, turned around, landed, and took off from San Lorenzo just before the torrential downpour made it impossible to see the end of the runway. After the rest of the team landed in Yurimaguas, we rented a bus and not just any bus, the "Death Ride Bus in the Dark through the Mountains."

Clean water wasn't always the only solution to keeping people healthy.

It seemed our bus driver had no concerns about his passengers. He spent most of the 80 miles of twisty, turny, 180-degree, blind switchbacks staring down at his radio trying to find a station that either had something he wanted to listen to or had a signal strong enough to last more than two minutes in the high mountains. It took us less than three hours to cover those 80 miles. When we got to Tarapoto, I looked at my dad and saw that he was about as pale and nauseated as I'd ever seen him.

Then began the 11 p.m. search for a hotel. After three attempts, we found one. Mom and Isabelle went out to find some dinner with Alison and Rosio. The rest of us were too tired to eat and went to bed falling asleep the minute our heads hit the pillow.

We woke up early to have a leisurely breakfast. But Jorge appeared and urgently reported that our plane was not leaving in two hours, it was leaving in 20 minutes! We grabbed our gear, hailed some tuk-tuks, and as fast as a moped can take you somewhere, we raced to the airport...and then we sat around for two hours waiting to take off. We were the last people to board our plane and had the first leisurely, calm ride for the first time in days as we headed back toward Lima.

• • •

Antarctica

Katherine

As a high school sophomore, I've traveled to all seven continents. Education is incredibly important to me. My parents have always made sure I value and appreciate it. My love of education may have been one of the driving factors behind why I got so mad when I was 5 years old to learn that girls my age didn't get to go to school because they were hauling water all day and the boys did. So when my parents began talking about taking a year off school to travel the world, I thought they had gone crazy. Looking back, I realize that the education I received in those 8 months was far richer than anything I could have learned at any school in 5th grade. Back home at Providence I missed learning about Phoenician culture but instead, I learned about the different South American cultures both native and European. I learned about the multitude of African cultures and saw firsthand the long-term ramifications of colonization. I learned history in the many, many museums we visited and science as well. We saw the last pods of pink freshwater river dolphins and the last of the giant river otters and leopards mating in the wild and 5 cheetah pups and their mother. I picked up a bit of language in every country we visited and music and art were easy to come by. Paper for Water has allowed me to travel and be a part of so many incredible things. During our trip, we visited a lot of water projects, but we also went to places just because they were on our bucket list.

After Peru, my family had traveled to Chile to meet up with some good friends of ours who live in Dallas. Before we'd left for the trip, we'd packed a giant suitcase of extra jackets, long underwear, and ski pants and left it at their house so when they met up with us, they could bring it and we didn't have to carry it the whole time. We'd definitely need it where we were headed next… Antarctica!

We started our Antarctic expedition in Punta Arenas, a small town at the southern end of Chile. From there, the captain navigated us through the channel, down the Strait of Magellan, down toward Cape Horn. I was in awe as we went through the fjords. There were tons of giant glaciers. Honestly, it looked a lot like Norway or another Scandinavian country. It blew my mind that I was seeing them in South America. Everything was smooth sailing until we crossed The Drake Passage. It was here that we learned the wonders of Dramamine, a seasickness pill. Everyone, except Trinity and Dad, spent the majority of the 2-day crossing flat on our backs strapped into our beds trying to not hurl every 3 seconds. Trinity however had the time of her life. Completely unaffected, she ran all over the cruise ship making friends with all of the crew. She had the dining hall almost completely to herself and the empty hallways made a great race track, according to her.

After navigating the seasickness and going through channels, we crossed a large stretch of the sea until finally arriving at a peninsula. Every day while there, we woke up early, hopped on some Zodiacs, and ventured on a new excursion including several Antarctica bases. We'd either go on land in the morning and a boat ride in the afternoon or vice versa. Although it took some convincing, Dad and I signed up for a sea kayaking course while we were there too; I was the only kid who signed up. I was the youngest in the room by at least 15 years. We sat through hours of orientation learning just how fast you would die once submerged in the freezing water. Despite having a dry suit on, you'd only have about 15 or 20 minutes of extra time before losing all coordination, strength, and succumbing to hypothermia and death.

I think my least favorite part of the whole experience was having to put on the drysuits; It was a harrowing experience completed every morning before going out. They are similar to wet suits except, true to their name, they keep you completely dry. They have rubber feet and airtight seals around your wrists and neck. It was near impossible to pull the suit over my head because of how tight it was. Now I'm not claustrophobic, but I definitely was on the verge of a panic attack almost every time I tried to pull the suit on. You can't really blame me. It would get stuck halfway down my face and then I just couldn't pull it any further, giving me the sensation of suffocating. Aside from the drysuit, the kayaking was awesome. Once we were all suited up, we'd go on over to the shore and get our kayaks. The first day everyone had to attempt a cowboy-style recovery in their kayak. This simulates falling out of your kayak and getting back in. It might sound easy, but you have no idea how difficult it is! The second you fall into the water you are immediately freezing. While treading water and trying to keep as much of your body out of the water as possible, you then have to flip your kayak back over remembering to not let go of your paddle. This is almost impossible due to the fact that it is full of water and very heavy. It took me almost 10 minutes to flip it over and by then I was exhausted and shivering. Once flipped over, you have to then pull yourself into the kayak without tipping it back over. After many failed attempts to pull myself in, I finally got it! Believe it or not, I was the only person out of everyone who was kayaking, including my dad, who successfully completed the cowboy recovery. My dad tried for 15 minutes to get in his boat and the instructor finally had to force him to accept his assistance. I still brag about it to him sometimes because he can beat me in almost everything else. Near the end of each kayaking excursion, my feet would be numb and I would be exhausted. But I loved the feeling of the boat gliding and the sound my paddles made. In retrospect, maybe it was a foretelling of my love for rowing.

One day, after watching tons of baby penguins along the shore, I decided to break the rules and build a snowman. I know, believe it or not, snowmen are illegal in Antarctica (at least according to the people who led our excursions). Packing the snow together and checking every so often to make sure no one would see me, I constructed a masterpiece. I carved some eyes and a mouth and then placed my hat and gloves on him. I was proud of him so I ran and got my dad to take a picture. I love that photo. My dad decided to take the opportunity and create a video with me while he had his camera out. He asked me to sit on the side of a snowbank and look around. Antarctica is the largest amount of freshwater of any continent in the world, it's just all frozen in ice. The icebergs there were insanely massive, dwarfing our large cruise ship. ninety-five percent of the world's freshwater is in Antarctica; however, global climate change is melting that ice and causing it to mix with the saltwater ocean. It was so awe-inspiring and at the same time upsetting to realize that the scenery I was looking at wouldn't still be there for all the generations of people after me to gaze at. Antarctica is changing rapidly and probably within a decade it won't look like it does today. The ice shelves are breaking off and the ice mass of the continent is decreasing daily. I talked about this briefly in a YouTube video for our channel. Unfortunately, that YouTube video has only 95 views, one of our least-watched videos. I wish more people would understand what is happening in the world in which they live.

When it came time to leave, we went back the way we came. Only this time, there was a massive storm with almost hurricane-force winds and six-story waves. With every wave, the boat would go up and then drop down about six stories. Then, it'd go back up and then drop down again. Rinse and repeat.

Dad has a crazy video of him standing on the sixth-floor deck at the front of the boat with Trinity where you can see the waves splashing up six stories. These were 40 to 50 foot waves! It's crazy to think that Shackleton's boats were about a quarter the size of our big cruise ship. In 40 to 50 foot waves, their entire boat would have been drenched with each wave that crested. It's hard to imagine those men spending months wet and cold. Those explorers were a different breed of men. Despite the hardships of this trip, we all want to go back to Antarctica. I want to go back with my dad and climb Mt. Vinson, which might provide some good chapters for our next book.

• • •

The Fall, Buenos Aires

Katherine

I think my dad tells the story about "The Fall" in Buenos Aires so much better than I do, but I'm going to try. At this point in our Around-the-World Adventure of 2017, we'd returned from Antarctica and had visited several countries in South America.

At least for me, I'd reached the point where the trip was wearing on me a bit. Being gone, not seeing friends and family, and wearing the same clothes for three months had gotten a little old. The trip had kind of transitioned out of feeling like summer vacation or a long spring break into just these endless travels. I felt tired, but I was ready to go to Africa. I thought the change of scenery would be exciting and rev me up again.

At the same time back home, my great-grandfather, who was in his 90s, experienced a stroke. We didn't know if he'd be OK, if mom needed to go say goodbye, or even if she could make it home in time, but wanting to be there with him, my mom decided she needed to fly back to the United States. So, suddenly, my dad was going to be traveling to Africa alone with us three young girls, which wouldn't normally be a problem. It's a little bit more complicated when there's only one parent and you are flying to South Africa. It has strict rules about only one parent traveling with children to prevent child trafficking and parental kidnapping. Since mom was leaving, she and Dad had gone to the US Embassy for an emergency appointment to get the required paperwork. (Be sure to ask my mom about the miraculous way the appointment came about.) The next morning with paperwork in hand, Dad and the three of us headed to the airport. We got to the airport and were checking in at the counter and handing over all the paperwork. Imagine our surprise when the guy at the desk said, "You're missing a document. You don't have everything you need."

"What are we missing?" my dad asked, panic creeping into his voice. He had checked the website carefully and even then was pulling up the website on his phone to show the counter guy.

"Notarized copy of their mother's passport," he said.

Oh, wow.

Dad pointed out to the counter guy that there was nothing on the website requiring this, but he was adamant. So we called my mom, a bit frantically and pleaded with her, "Mom, Mom, we need this, we can't go on our flight without this, we literally can't leave without this, can you get this?"

Back at the hotel, Mom was fully packed and about to head to an art museum and to lunch with some friends she'd made on our trip to Antarctica before going to the airport for an evening flight home. Listening to Dad frantically explain our situation, she suddenly remembered that just the day before we had walked past a notary school. Being a notary in Latin culture is *completely* different than in the United States. It's a really big deal and a coveted position. In some countries, the honor must even be inherited. She knew it was nearby, but not exactly sure where. She quickly took her luggage to be stored downstairs and asked for a hand-drawn map to the school. Running most of the way she arrived out of breath and sweating at the school information desk. After struggling to communicate she learned that they train notaries but that they weren't actually able to notarize anything. So after getting the address for a notary a few blocks away, she was off and running again. Entering the door at the address, the hall was quiet and she pulled the accordion metal screen door open to an old elevator and went upstairs. No one, absolutely no one was at work in one single office in the building. Reversing her way downstairs and walking discouraged out to the sidewalk, the doorman informed her that the earliest anyone ever came to work was 11:00 a.m. By now we were resigned to the fact that we were going to miss our flight. Mom called Dad and said she was hopping on a bus back to the embassy in hopes of getting what was needed. Dad said we'd head back to the hotel to regroup. I want to let you know that the remainder of this story is abbreviated and if you want the full tale that includes my parents going to the South African Embassy and mom losing her passport you'll need to ask her.

At the US Embassy, Mom didn't have a special emergency appointment like the day before, so she had to wait in line with hundreds of other people. Finally, she had the notarized birth certificate in hand, and as she was paying the fee, the embassy staff member assisting her mentioned the required transit visa for Brazil. Knowing it could take months for a visa, Mom didn't say a word but said a silent prayer that we wouldn't be asked for our visas.

Meanwhile, my sisters, Dad, and I had rebooked our tickets and arrived back at the hotel thinking, this is a chance to get a good night's sleep. We would wake up, have a nice, lazy breakfast, and make our flight. It would all be smooth and relaxed. Well, famous last words. First of all, the hotel was completely booked. After saying bye to mom, who was heading to the airport, we now needed to find somewhere else to stay. Luckily our dad was pretty good at that, and we were soon headed to another hotel.

So, I got up the next day following Dad's policy that we always get to the airport two hours early. If it's a domestic flight, maybe there's a little wiggle room, but for an international flight, we always arrive two hours early. The number of times we have shown up to go somewhere, not knowing we needed visas or having left without our passports, has stamped into him that two hours is the minimum our family can have. He had called for a taxi cab the night before, and it showed up on time. It looked a little small from the outside, but Dad didn't seem too concerned until he opened the trunk to put our bags in and saw that the entire trunk was filled with a propane tank. It literally had no trunk. So we piled all our bags inside the vehicle and then squeezed in on top of them. Dad had his bag under his feet and basically had his knees up to his chest. It was like a clown car.

We arrived two hours early and leisurely made our way to the same ticket counter as the day before. This time, the guy said, "You don't have a ticket for this flight."

"What do you mean? Yes, of course, we do. Our travel agent sent us the tickets," Dad said and started to pull them up on his phone.

That's the moment we realized that we were standing in line for the wrong airline.

"What do I do?" asked my dad, trying to communicate in the little Spanish that he knew.

The guy at the desk started talking to someone else who worked for the other airline. They were going back and forth in Spanish, and he sent us down to another counter. The lady there quickly checked us in and then got on her walkie-talkie. Suddenly, she turned to us and said, "Go! You guys need to go. Your flight leaves in ten minutes."

Now may be a good time to mention that we had been traveling with one carry-on suitcase and a large hiking backpack each. Only my backpack probably weighed as much as my suitcase did. I'd crammed in a bunch of stuff, and because space was so limited, my hiking boots didn't fit, and I had to wear them on travel days and when we flew.

I hated those hiking boots prior to this event, and well, now I hate them even more. They were uncomfortable, probably because I never actually wore them enough to break them in. So, to paint the full picture, there I was in hiking boots with a massive backpack and roller bag. I also never fully tied my hiking boots. The laces were loosely looped around the back of the boot and then stuffed into the shoe. I'm not super stupid or incompetent as far as tying shoes goes, I just never fully committed to the actual tying part.

Running and hoping to clear security and immigration in ten minutes, the laces were loose and flying down the corridor with me. Well, I tripped over the shoelaces and wiped out. I went to catch myself, but one hand was on my backpack, and one was on my suitcase. Without any hands to break my fall, I caught myself with my face. With a total faceplant down, I hit my chin. My wrist was crushed under the weight of my body and my knee was banged up. My dad rushed beside me. "Are you okay?"

I felt disoriented, but I tried to get up. Blood gushing from my mouth and chin, I said, "I'm fine… I'm fine."

Fine rarely means fine, but I knew we had a plane to catch. So we kept going. The security guy eyeballed us because can you imagine anything else that screams child trafficking more? Here's an older guy leaving the country with three young girls, one of which clearly looks injured and another that looks nothing like him. (I've always joked Trinity is the adopted one because of her bright blonde hair.) But he didn't stop us. So I ran to the gate with the stupid hiking boots still on. My knee was super swollen, and I was trying to stifle my sobs. We arrived at the gate huffing and puffing and were ready to board when we discovered that the plane had been delayed two hours.

Wow, that whole stupid rushing thing was completely unnecessary.

Since my dad is a doctor, he always has medical stuff on him when we travel. Isabelle pulled out an ACE bandage while he gave me tons of Tylenol and started to assess my injuries, "Well, you don't need stitches, Katherine, but you did chip a tooth."

I immediately stood up ignoring the burning sensation in my knee and found the nearest bathroom. I stared at myself in the mirror for a few moments taking in my swollen appearance and a badly chipped tooth.

Great. No, just wonderful.

I washed as much blood off as I could and then made my way back to our gate. My dad came up to me to ask how I was doing. I just shrugged my shoulders. He waited a moment before asking, "Do you want to go home to Dallas? It's an option."

"No, no, let's go," I said. "We've been looking forward to this trip forever. Africa is next. We need to keep going."

Through it all, Dad kept up such a strong exterior. I'd later find out that this was his weak moment of the trip where he thought about going back. He'd weighed out whether we'd had enough worldly experiences, whether we should return home or continue without Mom.

We decided to continue on our travels. To be honest, I was miserable the whole time it took to get to Cape Town. My face was swollen and throbbing so much I couldn't eat or sleep. When we got to Brazil for our layover, the airport was massive, and we walked for an insanely long time. I don't know if I've ever walked that much in an airport, and that's saying something. On the bright side, no one asked us for our transit visas thank God. When we arrived in South Africa, Trinity came down with something and her tonsils got super swollen. My dad was debating taking her to a hospital and was also trying to keep me comfortable. He was having a rough time.

Crazy things happen. Stuff doesn't always go according to the plan, and you have to decide to keep going. We literally weathered the storm coming out of Antarctica and had to weather the storm in an entirely different sense going into Africa. Because we did so though, we ended up with incredible experiences over the next five months that we would have missed if we had given up and gone home.

• • •

Zimbabwe

Katherine

Dad, Isabelle, Trinity, and I visited the Wine Country and the Southern Coast of South Africa while Mom was back in the States with her grandfather, who was recovering from the stroke he had while we were in Argentina. The whole family got back together in Cape Town after we had been apart for two weeks. Mom would have come sooner but got so sick with vertigo that she couldn't fly.

It was good to have the family back together, and we hiked the Wild Coast together with Will and Brandy, who had helped plan our trip, and our new friend Leigh. The history of the Wild Coast is intense, crazy, mysterious, murderous, and beautiful. They say that the Wild Coast has more shipwrecks per square mile of coastline than any other place in the world. It's located where the warm water of the Indian Ocean meets the cold water of the Arctic Ocean. Weather patterns and ocean currents collide to create danger, but the remoteness and the inaccessibility create a pristine environment that is beautiful and amazing for hiking.

From South Africa, we flew into Harare, Zimbabwe. Getting there from the east coast of South Africa was an experience in and of itself. We had flights canceled because of a South African Airlines strike and were delayed eight or ten hours, but when we arrived, the Living Water International team was waiting with smiles and balloons for Trinity. It was incredibly late at night, probably after midnight as we drove through the streets of Harare to our hotel.

Zimbabwe, like so many African countries, has had a difficult colonial history. Liberation from the British Empire and subsequent self-rule hasn't been great for Zimbabwe with a lot of governmental abuses from a long-reigning dictator. There is a lot of poverty in Zimbabwe and hyperinflation, but as in most countries we traveled in, the people were so kind and lovely to us.

Dad told me later that driving through the downtown area of Harare at night in the hotel's Range Rover was one of the scarier parts of the

Stuff doesn't always go according to the plan, and you have to decide to keep going.

trip. He was in the passenger seat where the windows weren't nearly as tinted as the back and he could see all the homeless people wandering the streets and approaching the vehicle at each traffic light. We checked into our hotel and as soon as our heads hit the pillow, we were asleep. The next day, we met the whole Zimbabwe Living Water Leadership Team, and they explained our itinerary. Soon, we hopped in a van and headed out with a police escort to the countryside to visit our water projects. On our way to our first school, we passed by these amazing rock formations. They were these huge rocks literally the size of giant houses stacked on top of each other out in the middle of otherwise flat terrain. It was totally bizarre.

At the first school, we took a little tour and learned that a Buddhist temple in Taiwan had decided to help fund the construction of the classrooms. It was an interesting intersection of faiths and one that we hadn't seen before. Most Zimbabweans are Christian including Protestants, Catholics, Evangelicals, the Zion Christian Church that still observed all Old Testament food laws, and some very conservative Christian groups that were still practicing polygamy. It was our first taste of Christianity that was very different from what we were used to and it was honestly kind of shocking. Here at home, we have so many social safety nets, but in some places around the world marrying again might be the only way to keep yourself and your children from starving. I'm not advocating polygamy, but I saw it in a whole new light. I was grateful for safety programs at home that help feed and care for people going through tough times and give women and children options and freedom from desperate choices.

This was the first school we had been to in Africa, and we had one last soccer ball from the Dallas Fossil team to give out, so we gave the ball to the principal of the school. I don't think we've talked about the amazing partnership that started back in 2014 with Fossil, the watch company. They had a sustainability project using scraps from making leather purses and wallets and were using those colorful leather swatches to make soccer balls. Anyway, the principal was so excited to receive the ball that she had all the students pose for a picture with Isabelle, Trinity, me, and the soccer ball. It's one of our favorite pictures because everyone is so happy!

We briefly mentioned this earlier, but there's an entire process for a community getting a water project. To summarize quickly, the community first petitions Living Water International for a well. Next Living Water assesses the community and needs. This includes an assortment of things such as topography, where the water table is, and the type of well system needed. Additional considerations are made concerning the need for taps, latrines, and a possible water kiosk or electric pump. Before an installation, classes are held with the community on how to build latrines, best sanitation practices, and how to stop diarrhea with a sugar and salt mixture. They'll go over basic germ theory and the importance of washing hands and buckets. Then, they drill the well and get the community involved to help out. One person is designated as the water caretaker and learns how to repair and maintain the well.

The whole community can access the well. Everyone can have the water—all genders, all religions, all races. Most communities also pay a tiny price for the water, and that money helps pay for parts or repairs and in some instances electricity to run a pump. Living Water stays actively involved with the community for at least two years after the well is drilled to monitor water quality so it is safe to drink as well as ensuring it is well maintained and the community is practicing safe sanitation and hygiene.

Zimbabwe reminded me of the receptivity we'd experienced in India. Most of the people who lived there came out to meet us. One community, dressed all in white, welcomed us with traditional dancing and singing. Living Water partners with a local organization that has an incredible relationship with the local government. We went to several churches and government buildings and talked to the people who were working there. At schools and churches, Isabelle and I taught children how to fold origami. Kids performed skits and plays that included reenactments of their lives before and after having water. We'd never seen anyone perform skits like these. One of the scenes included hauling water to the hospital, which I'd soon learn more about.

From the school, we left for a governmental office north of Harare. We met with a local politician and had our picture taken with her. She was strikingly tall and beautiful, dressed in traditional Zimbabwe clothing. She sat down with us and told us about their partnerships with Evangelical Fellowship Zimbabwe and LWI and the success of the water projects. She gave us a preview of a hospital that we were going to go see and this seemed to excite Dad as he always loves to visit hospitals and talk to doctors and nurses around the world.

We got back in the van and drove a long time on dirt roads full of large potholes to a remote hospital. For years, it had functioned as a rural hospital, but despite having electricity, it had never had running water. We met a nurse there who talked to us about the hospital and about the water project that we had funded. She said the hospital was a maternity hospital. If you went to that hospital, you or your family members had to bring your own water. Can you imagine asking a pregnant mother to bring a bucket of water when she had her baby!

Even now, the well isn't connected to the hospital, but it is much closer. It has completely transformed the operations because while they may not have running water, at least they have clean water and

Once the water project was finished, the infant mortality rate in the hospital dropped significantly.

they have as much water as they need. The nurses and doctors were so grateful that they could properly clean and take care of people and their hospital rooms. It had completely changed the way that they were able to take care of people. That was the craziest thing that we saw when we were there, I think especially for my dad because he's a doctor.

Many people from the community had come to the hospital to deliver their babies, but until the water project was completed, their infant mortality rate had been the same as the rate for deliveries by midwives in the mother's home. It was hard to imagine a delivery room that couldn't be cleaned with running water between deliveries or that infants couldn't be bathed with clean water after being delivered. But once the water project was finished, the infant mortality rate in the hospital dropped significantly.

These are the kind of stories with real-world outcomes that we live for! Projects that have an immediate impact get us excited.

It's interesting that often we get asked this question about saving infant lives. People say, "Aren't you contributing to overpopulation and just creating more of a problem in the future with more people that need to be fed?"

Here's what we've learned. Clean water empowers communities. Each year, 240 billion hours are wasted hauling water from up to seven miles away in the dry season. It primarily affects women and young girls. If you can repurpose that time into going to school or to planting a garden or starting a business, you elevate the financial security of a community. As the financial security of a community increases, the birth rate decreases. In addition, keeping young girls in school longer results in marriage at later ages and naturally reduces the number of childbirths.

• • •

Ethiopia

Katherine

Ethiopia was probably Isabelle's least favorite country that we visited, and if I'm being completely honest, I really wanted it to be our favorite because Ethiopia is the home of our very first water project. Unfortunately, we were not able to actually visit that original one because there was some major tribal conflict. While it wasn't safe to go to that well, we were able to visit a lot of other projects in the area around the capital.

It's interesting though. Ethiopia is a beautiful country and has such a rich history, but it was one of the few places on the trip where I felt unsafe. Maybe it was the fact that we stood out so much as we walked around in shorts and shirts. Or maybe it was the warning from the State Department saying, *"Don't travel to Ethiopia,"* but, hey, I guess we are adventurous! Most nice buildings, and our hotels, had armed guards. There were guards with AK 47s at the airport, in parking lots, and everywhere. It was a bit surreal and just kind of scary. But despite all of that, I am so glad we went because it was an eye-opening experience. It was definitely worth visiting because of the interactions with the people. My mom, however, *loved* Ethiopia, its food, its history, its castles, and its diverse cultures.

Ethiopia has so much natural beauty, but sadly a lot of it is being devastated by the people. People were cutting down trees to use as firewood because they don't have electricity or any other form of fuel. There's an insane amount of pollution because people burn plastic and basically whatever they can find for fuel. The emissions on cars also aren't regulated. So you could definitely say it was the least developed country we visited in Africa. The poverty level reminded us of our visit to India and the average monthly wage was equivalent to only US$20. Travel was often by donkey or horse-drawn wagon in the countryside. It was almost like going back in time.

Ethiopia was definitely a place where I saw the difference that having a well in the village made. While we were there, I visited a village and met a woman who had lost three kids because of the water. I actually saw their original water source, which was basically a hole in the ground with steep, crumbly sides of dirt. If you got too close, you could easily fall into the well. Not only was it dangerous, but it was really dirty. Before the community received the new well, the women had to strain their water through cloth to remove green worms from the water. They couldn't get all of the larva, eggs, and bacteria that were in the water though. She'd lost three children from that water. She went on to say that since she has had access to the new well, no more of her children had died but were healthy and getting an education. All because they now have clean water.

Her story would become one I'd tell all the time. It's dramatic, but it was the truth. Interacting with the woman was kind of like hearing about a rainbow after the storm. She went through this awful, tragic experience, but now her kids were happy, healthy, and able to go to school. Isabelle and I got to witness the real impact and hear firsthand about the lives saved because of the work we were doing with **Paper for Water**.

Our trip to Ethiopia was an interesting and powerful experience. My dad has a good friend who is Ethiopian and lives in Dallas, and while we were there, we were able to meet his friend's brother, who ran a school

She went on to say that since she has had access to the new well, no more of her children had died but were healthy and getting an education.

there. So we visited, met school kids, and talked to them, which was really neat. The day we visited was a Saturday, and the girls were there learning about sanitation and making homemade washable sanitary napkins. The school was mainly funded by the Korean government and provided lunch to its students as well as students from surrounding schools. We toured the kitchen that prepared meals for hundreds of children during the week. The school was surrounded by trees and a garden growing both food and flowers.

The hotel where we were staying had a hair salon and for the first time on the trip, we all got our hair cut. It was a very nice place and I'm sure more expensive than a regular salon, but the crazy thing was that for all five of our haircuts with tips, it was only thirty bucks!

Another thing that boggled my mind was how they were doing their state or countrywide, standardized testing for college admissions. I think the year prior they had a major test scandal with answers being leaked over the internet. Their solution? Turn off the internet for the entire country.

It was insane to me. I think there'd be rioting in the streets if the government turned off all of our internet! I think there may have been some protests, but nothing big. Everyone just went on with it. It didn't seem shocking to them. When we tried to check in for our departing flight, we couldn't access the internet because there was none in the whole country. Instead, we drove to the airport and hoped for the best.

• • •

Kenya

Katherine

Sometimes, our Africa trip blurs together, but I think we'd been traveling for five months at this point, and our grandparents came and met up with us in Kenya. It'd been quite a while since we'd seen people that we knew. We'd met up with some church friends right before Antarctica and some cousins when we went to Valparaiso, Chile, and even saw some cousins who live in Cape Town. So it was great to see our grandparents and have them be in on part of the fun. They've been incredibly supportive over the years. They'd gone with us to India back in 2013 to see our water projects, they would go on the Disney cruise (that story is still to come), and they had attended most of the Living Water galas with us. I think it's safe to say, they are the number-one fans of **Paper for Water**. In addition to our grandparents, Scott and Stephanie Frost, longtime supporters of our project, and my mom's friend Katy joined our group. Mom and Katy had worked on the same program in Japan after college and she was now in the State

Department and flew to meet us from Romania. Katy was hilarious and kept us laughing constantly.

By the time we'd reached Kenya, Isabelle was the only one who hadn't gotten sick yet. We were doing some touristy things and had gone to a restaurant at the home of famed author Karen Blixen. She was talking with one of the people who we'd just met and was telling them, "We've had a lot of problems. But I'm the only person who hasn't gotten sick yet." It wasn't a statement, more like bragging, even accompanied by some teasing of how some of us had been sick multiple times.

Those were famous last words—she said it while eating and drinking some mango juice. Mom's phone received a Bible verse every day. She pulled out her phone and showed her that very day's verse—Proverbs 16:18. Pride goes before a fall.

Fast forward two hours: we were at a bead factory and while wandering around the gift shop, she turned green. "Dad, I don't feel well. Can we wrap it up and go back to the hotel?" she asked.

"Sure, we can do that," he said.

So we piled into our van. This van was ancient with no air conditioner. It wasn't well insulated and anything you smelled outside, you could smell inside. Remember, it was Africa in the middle of June, so it was horrendously hot. With no emissions regulations, all of these old vehicles were belching out toxic fumes all around me, including the van I was in. It smelled so bad. We inched along in stop-and-go traffic while Isabelle tried not to be sick in the back of the van. After a two-hour drive to the hotel, she promptly threw up and spent the next day in bed.

While getting sick is probably one of the most memorable things Isabelle remembers about Kenya, there were some pretty incredible moments too, like seeing the well-drilling rig. We saw it at one of the Living Water offices, which was really cool. I'd seen photos before, but I don't know if I'd ever seen one in actual life until that point. It was way bigger than I thought it'd be! I think my favorite project that we visited was the one where I got to meet the well caretaker and talk with him for a while. I'd known the basics of what Living Water did and how the process worked, but I never really knew the logistics of how they actually kept it working. I didn't realize that often a well also provided a job for someone. The well caretaker's salary comes from all the people who get water there. They pay a very, very small amount, and then that money pays for the salary. I think for a while I was confused why people would have to pay at all. I thought it was kind of a faulty system if that makes sense. For a while, that was my train of thought. But then I got to meet this well caretaker and when I talked with him, I realized how wonderful it was that this water project not only could sustain life and keep people healthy, but it could also provide a job for someone, which was an aspect that I had never really thought about—the well creating jobs.

This trip to Kenya was also notable for being the first international trip we had taken with donors. Our goal anytime we take volunteers

I realized how wonderful it was that this water project not only could sustain life and keep people healthy, but it could also provide a job for someone.

and donors to a water project is for them to see firsthand what having access to clean water does for a community. We spend a lot of time in the United States talking about how clean water is foundational to a community. You can't lift a village out of poverty if there isn't easy access to water. Time is wasted because kids are sick all the time and can't go to school and people die of waterborne diseases. The reasons are obvious but when you see it firsthand, our mission becomes contagious! The Frosts and Katy saw it in person and it moved them. Hospitals with declining death rates because the hospital staff could wash their hands between patients. Schools with almost 100 percent attendance because the children weren't hauling water all day and weren't homesick with waterborne diseases. These rural schools had students that were so in love with learning that they were continuing their education in college and churches were being built left and right and growing! It is so hard to preach about the love of God when there's no clean water to drink but you can easily talk about the Living Water of Christ when you just built a water project and brought clean water to a village for the first time ever. And what's even better is that you can circle back to the love of God when you show them that the gift of water is for everyone in that community. Not just Christians, but Muslims and Jews and Hindus and gay people and other marginalized people in Africa like albinos. All people deserve the love of God through clean water.

• • •

Uganda

Isabelle

As I mentioned before, we'd arranged to partner with Akola in Uganda to make some of the ornaments for Neiman Marcus. When my grandparents met up with us in Africa, they brought some of the paper that we'd be using for the partnership. And when we got to Uganda we met up with my grandma's cousin Bob Hanifen, who brought the rest. He also had a special care package from Mrs. Sinasac filled with letters from our school friends. We read them over and over again.

Akola means "she works" in a local Ugandan dialect, and I was excited to get to interact and work alongside the women who work with Akola. When we first arrived in Uganda in June, we traveled to visit a very special water project at a school next to the Bwindi Impenetrable Forest National Park. We spent the day meeting and playing with the school children and of course teaching them origami. Two wonderful Dallas women, Carol Doggett and Deborah Cliff worked tirelessly to help bring this project into reality. It was rewarding to see the major impact it had had on the school and the community. Our next stop was the Akola headquarters in Jinja, several hours drive from Kampala, the capital of Uganda.

Over the next week, we taught the women how to fold and helped them make as many ornaments as possible. Unfortunately, we ran into a few problems. The biggest problem was that the Caspari paper had been cut so badly that it wasn't even close to being square. And when you're teaching someone who has no idea how to fold for the first time, you need square paper because they don't know how to adjust for a paper that isn't square.

Nobody had looked at or examined the paper beforehand. I think we'd assumed the paper would be fine since it'd been cut at a Dallas FedEx shop. But when I went to teach a group of women, I looked at it and thought, *Oh no, oh my gosh, this is wrong, this is not good.* So every evening after that, we sat in our hotel and individually tried to correct every single piece of paper. It was so horrible. Thankfully the family that owned the hotel where we were staying pitched in for hours nearly every night helping us.

And while the women were very talented at making beads, they were not particularly great at folding. Not because they couldn't be, it was just that a lot of them needed glasses. When rolling beads, you can touch and feel it, you can tell, *Oh, it's round, we're good.* With paper, you need to be able to see the line that you're folding to. Yet, they couldn't see any of the lines. We certainly hadn't taken that into consideration at all. Because of that, there were a lot of quality control issues. It ended up working out all right, more or less, but despite our long hours of folding, we weren't able to complete all of what needed to get folded there. So some of the work had to be completed by our volunteers in the US.

Aside from that, the best part of working with Akola was being able to meet the women and see how they'd been empowered. I toured the community and visited some of the women's homes. At one of their homes, a woman pointed out that she'd been able to buy an actual small glass window pane, which was really significant. Another woman bought a cow with the money that she'd saved. It was incredible to witness how they were working to get themselves out of poverty.

> *Often, I only focus on the bare necessities, which is obviously water. When a community gets water, it is amazing. But now, I realize there's so much more to do, and it was really impressive to witness and see how Akola is doing that. They're doing that next step, and we were able to work with another organization that was also helping to bring people out of poverty in another way.*

While traveling around the world, there was an incredible amount of work going on back home. In order to have everything ready for the Fantasy Gift and delivery of the store ornaments, we needed to complete everything by September 15th. Since we wouldn't be going home until the end of August, we relied heavily on our volunteers to complete everything while we were gone. They pulled through, but that's not to say it wasn't super stressful trying to manage the operation from another continent. I remember a lot of late-night calls with volunteers and Kayla, our VP of operations. In the midst of that process, we were also planning our annual event.

• • •

Isabelle

Our work for Neiman's didn't stop when we took off for our trip around the world. The $50 fantasy gift ornament hadn't even been finalized. On the Trans-Siberian Express from Moscow to Mongolia, I brainstormed with my mom and sister on the type of ornament to make and we experimented with the design. We got help from one of our favorite origami designers and all-around great person, Ekaterina Lukasheva. She helped us through email exchanges when we had access to the internet. She is a true genius and has published several origami books and has helped us with countless projects.

We then needed just the right paper because this was going to be a limited edition fantasy gift. It had to be special and exclusive. The search was on as soon as we made our way to Beijing after a visit to Mongolia. We combed market after market for paper, special beads, and tassels. In a jewelry shop near the pearl market, we met a friendly designer who ended up helping us by making tassels for a few of our designs. The rest of the ornament tassels were all made by hand by our Dallas volunteers. We still hadn't found "the" paper and we were feeling the pressure of the looming photography deadline for the Christmas catalog. Our next stop was Korea—paper paradise. Oh my, how would we ever choose? Searching for hours we finally found the perfect paper. The second I saw it, I thought, *This is it. This is the paper.*

Now we needed to get a sample to Neimans for photography. My mom expressed some of the paper to Dallas to some trusted volunteers, the Wisley family. They were familiar with many of Ekaterina's designs and we knew they would do a great job with the sample for photography. We hand-carried the rolls of paper we would need to create all the limited edition ornaments. We couldn't risk mailing it and as soon as we got home, we went into overdrive, working long hours so that we could deliver on time.

Soon after we made our warehouse delivery, our ornaments were shipped to every single Neiman Marcus store in the country. Then the fun began. We participated in a launch party and lots of interviews for articles and TV pieces to promote both our ornaments and our Fantasy Gifts.

It was exciting to see our pieces in one of the most famous stores in the country. Not only that but I learned a lot about the retail industry. Working with Neiman Marcus was an amazing opportunity, and through them, so many doors have opened for us.

• • •

Korea & Japan

Katherine

I'm sure by now you've seen God's ever-present hand on our project, opening doors we didn't realize needed to be opened and introducing people into our lives years before making their connection known, but nowhere is the Grand Strategist's presence over generations felt more than in Korea and Japan.

My dad was born in Japan and is half Japanese, but my dad's dad, Grandpa George, was born in Taegu, Korea, in 1907. Yes, you read that right, 1907, and yes, he'd be 114 if he were alive at the publishing of this book. Grandpa George was sixty-five when Dad was born, but that's for another book, possibly one that Dad will write someday in the future. Grandpa George wasn't quite Abraham, but he was old! We never met him because he passed away two years before Isabelle was born.

Now, Grandpa George's father was Great-Grandpa James Edward Adams. He arrived in Korea in 1895 and proceeded to plant over sixty churches around the southern end of the then United Korean peninsula. Almost all those churches still exist today and ten of them are megachurches with average Sunday attendance in excess of 6,000 members.

Grandpa George wasn't quite so successful with church plants, but he planted something just as important, apple orchards. The orchards helped the Korean people survive the brutal years after the Korean War. My grandfather was intimately concerned about feeding the needy and providing them with the Word, and I'm sure that his life work of horticulture and evangelism instilled in my dad the importance of feeding and watering His sheep.

Isabelle and I had never been to Korea before, so we had no idea what to expect. After shopping for paper and visiting some friends we left Seoul and traveled down the peninsula towards Japan to visit some of the churches my Great-Grandpa James had planted. And *oh my gosh!* We were treated like royalty! It was as if we had started the churches ourselves.

My mom made a comment that struck a chord with me, "*Your grandparents did so much that you are now receiving the blessings of that work. How can you live your life so that your grandchildren will receive that kind of welcome? How can you make the kind of impact that reaches generations?*"

They paraded us up on stage during one of their worship services—in the clothes that we had just spent the last seven months traveling around the world. I definitely felt underdressed and maybe even a bit grubby. They asked my dad to get up and speak. It was nice to see him have to think quickly on his feet the way Isabelle and I have had to when the people interviewing us ask unusual questions. I don't know if we get our comfort in front of the camera from him or if he's been around us so much that we've rubbed off on him, but regardless, he didn't embarrass the family and hopefully made the attendees feel the love we had for them.

Some of the elders of one church took us to a library dedicated to the early beginnings of their church. We learned about these four faithful women who prayed every day for a church to be built and were the backbone of the church's incredible growth. Planted in 1900, the church didn't really take off into megachurch status until the 1970s, but the original four faithful women didn't live to see it. It made me think how we were so fortunate to actually be able to see the growth of PFW. It's amazing to see the fruits of our labor during our lifetime because not everyone is given that gift.

From Korea, we traveled to Japan, starting with the island of Kyushu, where Dad was born in the city of Sasebo. Grandpa George had been a missionary there too. We stayed for a few days on Kyushu before traveling to the main island of Honshu and stopped in Nagoya, where one of my mom's friends, Megumi, lives. Megumi had been mom's homestay sister during a trip to Japan in college.

We stayed with Megumi and her family for several days. Megumi runs an English school, and Isabelle and I taught some of her students. Megumi arranged an afternoon folding party at the local municipal building and got 30 to 40 parents and kids to attend. We told the families about **Paper for Water**'s mission and how we are trying to change the world through bringing clean water and the Word to the Thirsty.

As we started teaching the children, it became apparent that multiple children had never folded origami! *How was this possible? Japan is the birthplace of origami!*

Our dad grew up folding origami because his Japanese mother had taught him. Because of his early love of origami, he knew that when I was 5 years old, not only could I learn how to fold but that I too would love it. The parents told us that origami wasn't taught in school much anymore because everyone focused on teaching math, science, standardized testing. Some of the parents commented on how ironic it was for Americans to have found a love for this Japanese art form and be reintroducing it to their Japanese children. They expressed their gratitude both for teaching their children origami and also for teaching their children about the world water crisis and life for millions outside of Japan.

> *While it's easy to see how our introduction to Mrs. Halliday at her birthday party four years prior led to the sale of our Neiman Marcus Fantasy Gift, it takes some digging to see God's providence generations ago...from our great-great-grandfather running a station on the Underground Railroad inspiring our great grandfather to be a missionary in Korea, to our grandfather planting orchards all over Korea and our dad's desire to make sure that his children understood the impact that we could have in the world. My sister and I didn't just come up with this plan to help people in foreign lands: it's been percolating for hundreds of years and hopefully will continue to grow for generations to come.*

• • •

Neiman Marcus Prep Work for the Fantasy Gift

When we returned home from our crazy Around the World 8-month trip, we immediately got to work making sure that all the ornaments were ready for delivery. Because of our amazing volunteers who worked tirelessly while we were on the road, we were miraculously able to have all of the ornaments done on time for each delivery deadline. Thanks to Sister Agatha and other volunteers the $50,000 Fantasy Gift included over 400 incredible ornaments and a private lesson from our friend and origami master, Ekaterina Lukasheva. The less expensive $50 Fantasy Gifts were completed and all the other ornaments that would be sold in the Neiman's Christmas department were delivered.

When we delivered our ornaments to the Neiman Marcus warehouse, we had the chance to meet Frank Ramirez and his wonderful team that would be packing the ornaments to be shipped out to each store. We even got a tour of the fulfillment center and the technology they have

It's amazing to see the fruits of our labor during our lifetime because not everyone is given that gift.

for packing and shipping orders was impressive. What really made a big impression was that most of the employees we met had worked there for decades. We also visited every Neiman Marcus store in the DFW area, and even a store in Houston to see our ornaments or host a trunk show. It was the coolest thing ever, to have our ornaments and work in such a prestigious and fancy store. At some of the stores, we talked to employees working there and told them a little about **Paper for Water** and how to explain it to shoppers. So many of the employees gushed to us how much they loved the ornaments and commented on how pretty they were and of course, loved their impact on people's lives.

When it came closer to the holiday season and time for Nieman to do their media, we were part of their blitz and on TV so many times.

In November, I attended the big release party for the fantasy gifts at Park Place Premier Collection with my family. It was a bit surreal, but I remember walking around the dealership and sitting in one of the McLaren 720s, one of my absolute dream cars. Giant posters of each Fantasy Gift lined the walls with samples of the gifts enclosed in glass cases. A couple of ornaments were in one of these cases in front of our poster. Representatives from each company selling a gift were all there, and the press interviewed each one to get their stories. I talked to so many reporters that day, explaining over and over what Paper for Water does, what the fantasy gift would be, and exactly how the $50,000 would impact people.

Having a Fantasy Gift was truly epic and special. Seeing Paper For Water ornaments in stores was the best pat on the back. Over a year of work and dedication had gone into planning the Neiman Marcus Fantasy Gift, and store ornaments and the hard work had paid off. We actually ended up working with them for several years too.

• • •

Disney Holiday Special

Isabelle

With Nickelodeon and the Kleenex video, Katherine and I were starting to get the hang of this filming thing. However, we had no idea what was in store for us next. Turns out, our parents had a little trick up their sleeves!

Sometime shortly after returning home from our trip we were contacted about an interview for a new reality contest featuring entrepreneurs. We weren't exactly a fit, especially since it would require us to miss several weeks of school. The person who interviewed us said she'd keep an eye out for other opportunities. About a month later dad got a call about a top-secret opportunity and had to agree not to tell us the details. We'd have to travel somewhere and miss school for it, which had started to be a big hassle rather than a fun chance to get out of class.

Dad needed to see if it was worth missing school without spoiling the surprise.

"Would you consider doing a filming project if you had to miss school?" Dad asked.

"Nah, I'm not interested in missing any more school than I absolutely have to," I said to my parents.

"Well, what are you willing to miss school for?" Dad asked.

"What if you got asked to be on the Disney channel? Would you miss school for that?" said Mom.

"Like that's ever going to happen," I said.

"Of course, we'd totally miss school for Disney," said Katherine, rolling her eyes a bit because my mom always tells us we have to have good manners at the dinner table because we might have a meal at the White House someday. (My manners are great; Katherine just gets way more excited about food than I do.)

I forgot about that conversation until one Saturday morning. Katherine and I were at the barn riding horses when my mom picked us up and said, "Girls, great news! You get to have gyros for lunch. A film crew brought them for an interview at our house right now. They just want to talk to you to see if you might be a fit for a show."

What the heck? Film us in our sweaty riding clothes? For who?

We were not ready to do an interview at all but thought we'd have to buckle down and do it since they were already at our house. I didn't really know who it was for and my parents were pretty vague in their explanations. So the quick interview ended up being five hours that day. The last shot they wanted was of us walking out the front door as a family. When we opened the door to walk out, a giant present was sitting on the doormat.

"Open it," said my mom.

I opened it to find a snow globe of the Disney castle. Shaking it around, I thought, this is cool, but I don't really understand why they're making a big deal of a snow globe. I looked into the box again and noticed a card on the bottom in the shape of Mickey Mouse. I pulled it out and opened it to find, *"Congratulations, you're going on a Disney cruise!"*

When I read it, I didn't believe it. *Really? There's no way that's actually going to happen.*

My reaction was really lame because I thought it was fake. I truly didn't think it was real. So the big, "Oh my gosh, this is so awesome" reaction that the producers wanted completely didn't happen. At one point though, I turned to my mom and asked, "Is this real?"

She was crying again because she always cries. Nodding, she said, "Yes! We're leaving tomorrow."

"Ladies, we're going to need you to do this again," said the film crew. So we put everything back in the box, went back inside, opened the door, and did it all again with a lot more excitement. The director said, "Yeah, much better."

"I'm serious about leaving tomorrow. You need to pack right now."

It was a whirlwind. We had a church lock-in that night too. So after we finished filming, I think I had 20 minutes to pack before we left to go to church and spend the night. And then Sunday morning, right after church, we went straight to the airport and flew to Orlando. The next big surprise was that our grandparents were actually coming too and we met up with them in the Orlando airport. It was super awesome because Disney had paid not only for the five of us but for our grandparents as well and Papa had never been to Disney before.

Crazy early the next morning, we drove to the port because they wanted to start filming before the guests began boarding the ship. We were going on the Disney cruise and they wanted to film us for the "Disney Holiday Special" and capture our full Disney experience. They filmed us getting on the boat and took a bunch of other shots before the cruise actually left the port for The Bahamas. I think it was supposed to seem like we were already on the ship during the cruise because it was before the people on the previous cruise had disembarked. So they were still on the boat and made it look like the other guests.

On that same day, Katherine and I spent time hanging out with Ethan Wacker, one of the Disney Channel stars. While playing mini–golf and talking to him about **Paper for Water**, the crew just kept filming everything. They got so much footage and content, walking and talking around the ship. I don't think I even remember everything we did. I thought it was funny that we filmed for a week for an eight-minute video.

We filmed for so long that we ended up having to scramble through immigration! We had to get off the boat and go back on as passengers. Everyone else had already boarded the boat, and we were some of the last people to get on the boat before it left. While we were waiting to get on though, there was a rocket launch at Cape Canaveral, which was so beautiful to see.

The ship was awesome! I filled the afternoon off with activities, sliding down the water slide and swimming while my sisters checked out the kids' area. My grandma, mom, and I went to the theatre every single night to watch all of the shows. One of the best nights though was Halloween! The ship held a massive party on the top deck. Everyone was in costumes, and there were trick-or-treating stations all around the ship.

Our cruise went to the main island of The Bahamas for a day before going to Disney's private island. Of course, they filmed us some more there, snorkeling in the clear blue water. On the days we were filming, we filmed most of the day, but it did have some perks! One day, they opened the slides early for filming, which meant we got to slide down over and over with lines.

After the cruise, they gave us two-day hopper passes to all the parks at Disney World. The second afternoon we headed over to film at Animal Kingdom. We actually showed up a half-hour early to the place where we were supposed to be filming, which is really rare for us. We're almost never early. Since they were not ready for us, they said, "Why don't you guys go ride one of the rides and then come back?"

"Do we have time?" I asked.

Suddenly, our really early arrival didn't seem like enough time to squeeze in a ride. I didn't think there was any way we'd have the time before the shoot. The best rides had up to a two-hour wait.

"Don't worry about that. We're going to send one of our people with you to cut the line. Why don't you go ride the brand-new one?"

They'd recently opened the Pandora area, which is the land from the movie *Avatar,* and it had a new ride with at least a two-hour wait. We zipped through it in 20 minutes! It was the coolest thing ever, and the most amazing ride any of us had ever been on.

When it came time for us to go home, I kept replaying the entire trip in my mind. I think it's one of the coolest experiences with **Paper for Water**. I couldn't believe my parents were in on it from the beginning, but it turned out that Disney had told them to keep it a surprise, which is why we even had the conversation about what we'd be willing to miss school for in the first place! It was an amazing reward for working hard. Katherine often says that "when you give a lot you get a lot back and sometimes more than you gave." I know that this is true because we've experienced it so many times.

Over the years, **Paper for Water** *has provided some amazing opportunities for our family. We have been able to go to the most incredible places and meet the most interesting people, and this trip was one such opportunity. I think the best part for me though was the fact that our grandparents, especially my papa who had never been to Disney World before, also got to come with us. As special as it was for us, I am so grateful to the wonderful people at Disney who made that possible for them.*

• • •

National Youth Workers Conference— Memphis

Katherine

Remember the Webb family that Isabelle mentioned earlier, the people with One Year Road Trip? Well, they helped connect us to my biggest solo speaking event ever at the National Youth Workers Convention. When the convention asked them for a youth referral, they recommended us. Keep in mind they had traveled the United States for a whole year interviewing people and out of everyone, they said **Paper for Water.**

I thought it was incredible that they remembered and suggested us. Yes, *us*. Being solo for the speech, however, was not part of the original plan.

Now, my mom is super old-school and uses a paper planner for her schedule. I make fun of her for it all the time even though I have a flip phone, but that is a different story. My mom likes making handwritten lists and planning everything on paper. It's super easy to lose or misplace… or double book. To this day, this is one of the main arguments I use when I'm trying to convert her to a digital calendar on her computer.

Somehow, she mixed up the dates and scheduled Isabelle and me to speak in Memphis on the same weekend that our school had one of their main productions, Grandparents' Day. For Grandparents' Day, every grade performs some sort of poem or song they've learned, and in 2017, Isabelle apparently had a "big role" and a legit speaking part. Regardless, I begged her, "Isabelle, please, it's not that important."

"No. Are you kidding me?" She said, "I've been working on this for months."

"Come on, please; it can't be that important."

"No; you have to do this one on your own."

I eventually gave up and reckoned that I could do it by myself, but I was definitely not keen on the idea. It was going to be the biggest solo speaking gig I'd ever done. At that point, I'd done one or two media pieces for TV by myself, but that's a different situation because you're talking to the interviewer and a camera person. Those aren't that stressful. Stressful is speaking to a room full of 7,000 people! Now, I may be overshooting the number a little bit, but it certainly felt like 7,000 people even if it was in reality probably only 5,000. Regardless, it was a lot of people, thousands and thousands of people.

And then there was the actual speech to write. Speech writing is definitely not one of my favorite things to do. Isabelle usually helps me, but I sat down with my dad for this one. When we were writing the speech, he asked, "What do you want to say in your speech?"

Just thinking about the speech made me sweat. I could already feel my tongue sticking to the roof of my mouth. I knew it was best to be as prepared as possible, though.

He continued, "You have an incredible opportunity because you're presenting to a crowd that you don't usually talk to, and you can give a speech that you normally wouldn't."

He was right. This crowd included a bunch of youth workers, groups from churches, counselors, camp staff, and church-related groups, all people who interact with the youth on a daily or weekly basis. I didn't know it at the time, but Dad had also watched and been inspired by Simon Sinek, a guy who did a powerful TED talk on how great leaders inspire action. Little did I know that 4 years later I would be the kick-off speaker for Simon Sinek at another speaking engagement. But in his TED talk that has been viewed over 28M times, Simon explains how people buy into *why* you do something, not how you do it. Previously, we'd always talked about how we did what we did for **Paper for Water** and the impact we've had. For this one though, I centered the speech around why we do it. I think my speech kinda copied Simon Sinek's, but imitation is the highest form of flattery, right?

Before the event, the nerves crept into my dreams. I woke up in a cold sweat, having dreamt that I had cracked under the pressure in the spotlight on-stage and forgot all the words. I mean, Isabelle had always been there. Whenever one of us forgets a line or messes up, the other person always steps in and smooths it out. We've never actually failed badly. I don't think we've genuinely ever had a moment where both of us were stumped and panicking. This would be the first time I didn't have that support to give me peace of mind. And this was a massive crowd. It didn't help that I didn't have the entire thing memorized either. The night before the speech, I panicked, *Oh my gosh, I don't know this, I literally don't know all the words.*

Sometime in the early morning on the day of the speech, I locked it down, and before I knew it, I was standing backstage with my dad in Memphis. When I'm nervous, I get sweaty, and I'd already sweat through my shirt and my jeans. Irrationally, I figured everyone would be able to see how sweaty and nervous I was. My dad still laughs when he tells people about it. Right before I went on stage, I went up to my dad.

"Dad, I'm literally about to throw up," I told him. "They're going to take one look at me and see that I'm a fraud who only just memorized their speech. I'll probably trip on my way up too."

"Don't worry; you've got this, Katherine, just like we've been practicing for hours. You could do this in your sleep; you know it inside and out," he reassured.

Well, the lead-up was more panic-inducing than the actual thing. That audience ended up being one of the most supportive crowds I've ever encountered. Sometimes, you give a presentation to people and say something that you think will be a wow factor or will draw a laugh, like here's the part where you clap for me and here's where you chuckle, but then nobody moves or breathes and it's just plain awkward. This, thankfully, was definitely not that crowd. This crowd was on it. If I said something a little funny, they laughed like I had said something positively hilarious. They even gave me a standing ovation when I finished!

As far as actual delivery goes, it was a solid speech and probably one of my best. I felt pretty darn pleased and accomplished walking off the stage. I'd written this speech, flown all the way up there, and delivered it on my own.

It definitely boosted my confidence. And if I'm being totally honest, it gave me a bit of an ego boost—well, correction, a lot of an ego boost, and it was a little something to hold over Isabelle's head. We hadn't done We-Day yet, so when I got home, I teased her, "Man, that was the biggest in-person crowd for **Paper for Water** ever. And I did it all by myself."

Hey, she's good at everything. Just let me have my little moment.

National Youth Workers Convention

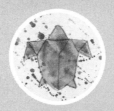

2018
OUR BIGGEST CHALLENGE YET

"Perseverance is not a long race;
it is many short races one after the other."
Walter Elliot

National Retail Federation Gala

Isabelle

> *The numbers make it real. When we first started in 2011 a child*
> *died every 15 seconds from lack of clean water and in 2018 that*
> *number had decreased to a child dying every 60 seconds. But that*
> *of course is still too many children dying. Think about that if you*
> *are reading this book at sixty seconds a page. Every page you turn,*
> *another child is lost. A family heartbroken and a community in*
> *mourning. We keep working because we know these numbers, what*
> *they were, are, and what they could become.*

January started with a hallmark, dream event—the most exciting one
we've ever been to by a long shot—one that allowed us to travel to
New York City for the first time since the United Nations Sustainability
Conference six years prior.

The National Retail Federation's Awards Gala spanned two nights. After we arrived in the city, we met up with Hedda for lunch at a really fun restaurant complex, Eataly. It was so special to meet up with her since she had connected us to Neiman Marcus, and our partnership with Nieman had led to this event. Karen Katz, the former CEO of the Neiman Marcus Group, who had worked with us and who loved our mission, served on the committee that nominated us for the Dreamer Award. At 14 and 12, we became the second-youngest recipients of the award.

Later that first evening, we attended the dinner for anyone who had ever won an award. As the only kids, it was awesome to get introduced to CEOs of major companies, and it gave us a great opportunity to talk to them. I remember having a long conversation with the CEO of Levi's about a possible collaboration.

People gave us more specific advice for being in the retail world, but there were a lot of encouraging conversations in general. I was a bit in awe that these leaders of industry were telling my sister and me that they were impressed with our efforts, that *we* were the ones doing such awesome stuff.

As much as I dislike relying on something external, the support of all these fashion industry leaders and the whole gala validated our efforts. To be there and to be participating with such accomplished adults struck a chord with me as if to say, "I do have a place. My voice matters. This isn't just some little kid's project. Other people recognize it as great too." To be in a space with all of these successful people and have them say what we were doing was really cool made me feel like the hard work was paying off to a point where influential people noticed.

Not knowing exactly where this mission will lead next is one of the fun aspects of being involved with the organization. Being open helps make it an adventure full of delights and surprises, and in this dinner's case, there were tables and tables of sweets, which felt like we'd arrived at our personal Willy Wonka candy buffet. Our younger sister Trinity took it to heart, and she even got "throw up" sick from eating too many red Twizzlers.

The dinner also included the most amazing silent auction. Walking next to the table, I tried to see if there was anything that **Paper for Water** could incorporate in the future and thought if we even come close to hosting an event like this in the future, that will be an incredible success.

I do have a place. My voice matters.

The next evening was the gala, our first real red-carpet event. As soon as we arrived, an assistant said, "Hand me your purse. Stand there, take a step, face the camera, and smile."

The experience felt surreal and special, almost like I was a celebrity. I inched my way down the line of photographers and thought, *if you had told me that I'd walk a red carpet when we'd started raising money, smiling for stock photos, I don't know if I would have believed you.* As the cameras snapped, I flashed to how just months earlier, Katherine and I'd had our boots on the ground in the hearts and homes of our water projects. With most of those being poor and destitute countries, the difference from there to where I stood was jarring.

Conversations at the gala evening seemed to center on how their company's success was linked to their ability to handle market volatility and that their financial strength came from being able to pivot rapidly during unpredictable times. While the conversation may have been more specifically geared toward the retail industry, Isabelle and I believe that adaptability and receptivity to change have been an undercurrent of **Paper for Water**'s success. By linking our success to the number of people we have helped, we have created a responsibility to those people and made the need to implement change bigger than us or any temporary discomfort.

At every event, I like to enjoy the present moment and see where I can also draw inspiration since it helps fill the well of ideas. While backstage before a small presentation, a college kid in a colorful bow tie walked by and said, "Y'all are going to crush it. Just learn and absorb as much as you can from the experience you're having now."

> *I realize now that was how we'd been taught to approach it all—as a learning experience. We value and understand the importance of schooling. It's part of what contributed to our desire to start the mission, to help allow other girls access to school instead of having to haul water or getting sick from unsafe water. Yet we also recognize the importance of seeing life and experience as one of the best teachers. So that's what we try to do—soak up all the knowledge like a sponge. The whole time we were working with Neiman, I viewed it as one giant learning experience, and this event arose from a part of that connection, another chance to learn.*

Everyone who won an award that night received an ornament from us. Instead of giving us our ornaments, the organizers gave us sunglasses that I have somehow managed not to lose. They came with a note that said, "Because your future's so bright." They also mailed all five of us large boxes of party swag, the best we'd ever received. The generosity still surprises me; who doesn't like a box of free goodies? Although I think one of the largest gifts of the event is how once you receive an award, you are given a lifetime invitation to a dinner for all past NRF winners. While there, Jim McIngvale of Mattress Mack stressed the importance of instilling a culture of empathy and giving back to the community. In future years, Isabelle and I may need to visit the dinner for just that type of networking and inspiration.

• • •

WE Day

Katherine

In the middle of March 2018, Isabelle and I arrived an hour early to sit for a fun hair and make-up experience for our largest speaking event ever. With freshly powdered faces, we walked to wait in a Green Room behind the giant television monitor and swirling lights backstage. My eyes followed a celebrity I recognized from *High School Musical* and Raini Rodriguez, an actress featured on The Disney Channel. I shook my head in a bit of disbelief.

Even though we'd been on the **Paper for Water** journey for seven years at this point, every now and then, there's a big event that awes me and makes me think, *Wow, we got HERE?!* From seeing the water projects in person and seeing the impact providing clean water makes to spreading the message and speaking in front of large groups, WE Day was one of those moments.

So there we stood in a sea of screens, wires, and speakers. On the other side, thousands of kids roared and cheered for a band playing for WE Day Texas, a community empowerment event for young change-

Every now and then, there's a big event that awes me and makes me think, *Wow, we got HERE?!*

makers whose collective volunteering efforts span the globe. None of the people cheering on the other side could even buy a ticket to this event; each attendee had to earn it with volunteer hours of service.

The organizers of the event had invited us to give a speech, and we'd spent hours prepping for this moment—the moment we'd replace the band playing on stage and speak to thousands of our peers. Thousands. I sorta hoped the kids would magically turn into adults. I'd always found adults to be easier to talk to than people my own age. By this point, we'd grown accustomed to speaking to a room full of adults but speaking to thousands of like-minded kids was proving to be a bit more nerve-wracking than anticipated.

I can't tell you if it was after five minutes or an hour, but at some point, a production assistant peeked her head into the Green Room and said, "All right, ten minutes ladies, ten minutes until you have to be on stage."

> *My mouth dried. My heart raced, matching the drumbeat of the sounds blaring from the loudspeakers.* **You're fine, you're fine. You've done this before. It's not going to be terrible,** *I thought, in an effort to give myself a pep talk.*
>
> **"You're fine, you're fine…."**
>
> *In those moments, I have to remind myself of the bigger* **why** *and make it not about my nerves. I have to remember that I'm speaking for the kids who cannot and that I am sharing the message with thousands of people, who could create their own butterfly effect flaps after hearing about our mission.*

The next thing I knew, Isabelle and I were weaving through the hustle and bustle of backstage like a pinball, dodging the people who were walking around with earpieces and talking into their walkie-talkies at a rapid pace.

As we jogged into the bright lights from the side stage, I smiled and waved at the audience. Even though I'm a runner, my mind kept thinking of the worst-case scenarios like, *Am I going to get on stage and be so out of breath that I'm not going to be able to start my speech?*

A spotlight followed our trail to the center platform, and when I reached the platform, I grabbed the microphone and focused my eyes on one teleprompter before scanning to the next. For a split second as my eyes crossed between the two, the people behind the screens came into view. Thousands of people. The words on the teleprompters were streaming too fast. My heart quickened.

I took a breath and trusted the preparation to take over. The nerves turned into confidence as I said, "A good friend had told us about the world water crisis. It was shocking to us that people had to leave their homes and travel long distances to fetch water...water that was probably dirty."

Isabelle chimed in, "After learning that, we decided we wanted to raise money to fund a well in Ethiopia...."

The crowd's energy shone throughout the arena, a palpable sense of compassion for our planet and all its inhabitants. The rest of the time on stage passed by in a blur. Offstage with the adrenaline pumping, I affectionately jostled Isabelle before embracing my mom. I couldn't help but shake my head, trying to understand what we'd been able to accomplish in the seven years since the **Paper for Water** journey began.

WE Day Texas

• • •

International Association of Fundraising Professionals Award

Katherine

Isabelle and I have had our fair share of highs and lows, but that doesn't mean we aren't still surprised when something doesn't go as planned.

Coming into April, riding a wave after the epic experience at WE Day in front of thousands of people, we were excited about our next speaking gig in New Orleans, especially since our grandparents were driving over from southeast Texas to be with us. Sometimes things go perfectly and sometimes we face obstacles and challenges. Maybe we should have known things might not go perfectly when we arrived at the airport and Katherine realized she had left her dress and shoes at home. Luckily there was a TJ Maxx near the airport, so that was our first stop before meeting up with our grandparents for a late dinner. The next day had a few more challenging surprises in store for us.

The Association of Fundraising Professionals (AFP) gave us our first award in 2012, and we were honored to receive an award from them again. But this time it wasn't a local chapter award, it was the International AFP award. For this award, we'd recruited Trinity to go on stage and give the speech with us. To be honest, Trinity wasn't even out of diapers when we'd started **Paper for Water**. I've felt bad making her do things because she never really had a choice in the matter. I honestly don't know if she's ever felt ownership even though she has come to most of our events and been supportive despite it not being her thing. She'd always loved the origami part of things, enjoyed making up her own folds and designs, and Isabelle and I had been jealous of her creative, artistic talent. For the longest time, she seemed disinterested in making videos or speaking, and looking back, I probably twisted her arm a little bit to agree to participate in the speech at the International AFP conference.

After arriving at the convention center for the awards ceremony, I stood backstage with Isabelle and Trinity waiting to present. Moments before the presentation, literally on the steps going up to the stage and right as the pre-stage jitters were setting in, the presenter began to announce the introduction to our segment, "The next honorees are a group of three sisters: Isabelle, Katherine, and Trinity Adams."
I was in my head, giving myself a pep-talk before the speech when two words came out of Trinity's mouth that interrupted my train of thought. She'd said, "Maybe not…."

She turned around and headed to walk off the stage, creating one of the most stressful moments of my entire life. My mind raced, thinking of how our three parts intertwined, analyzing whether we could do it without her. I locked eyes with Isabelle and realized that we hadn't memorized Trinity's part. We'd only memorized our portions, and like in a play, each of our lines cued the next person to speak.

"Wait," Isabelle said.

"What do you mean *'Maybe not,'* Trinity? You can't leave us hanging like this. You are going on that stage," I said, looking her in the eyes and placing my hands on her shoulders.

For a moment, I thought about us not going on stage, but that was never really an option. I admit, my last-minute pep-talk with Trinity was more of a stern, borderline threatening type of talk. What are big sisters for, right? She ended up going on stage with us after all, but with a frantic pulse beneath the presentation, we missed a whole section of the speech, which wasn't fabulous, but I doubt the audience truly noticed.

> *This was a huge lesson to make sure that everyone who is giving a speech is 100 percent onboard beforehand and to put in the work ahead of time to ensure full preparation. This experience triggered the realization that it isn't worth it to try and make anyone participate if they don't want to. There's also an element of matching actions or tasks with a person's interests.*

I discovered that everyone has different work styles and found if we tried to persuade Trinity to be a part of things that she didn't want to do, she wasn't as cooperative, and maybe rightfully so. However, if she delegated a task to herself, she was much more apt to complete it and be enthusiastic while doing it—like making videos for the YouTube channel. She enjoys doing those, which are great and a much-appreciated tool for social media.

Isabelle and I have worried about whether or not we'd be able to one day pass the torch to Trinity when our involvement with the organization evolves into a different role. Part of me thinks now that the reason she'd acted up then was that we hadn't given her a choice in the matter of involvement like our parents had always given us. Within the last two years, her uptake in involvement has made me over the moon.

After that stressful speech, we were leaving the convention center, and I was thinking we'd cleared the hurdle of the day, but the real disaster began after exiting the building. Having flown in the night before, we were on a tight schedule to catch a plane and had just enough time to make it to the airport. Scanning the parking lot, I noticed something amiss.

"Dad," I said, "…where's the rental car?"

"Dad, I have an exam tomorrow," said Isabelle.

His eyes widened. He started reading the lot's signage and scrambling for help. Mom stressed, and I could tell she was worked up but ready to spring into action mode too. Our plane was taking off in less than two hours. We barely had time to turn in our rental car and check-in and now we had to find our car, get it, and then go to the airport. Panic time!

"I'll call Grandma and see if they are still in the parking garage," said Mom.

Luckily, a man who had just heard us talk at the International AFP event came up to Dad and asked how he could help. He was there just at the right moment and was nice enough to drive him to an ATM and the impound lot where the car had been towed. All our luggage was in the car, so it wasn't like we could just abandon the rental car at the pound.

I've noticed that when bad things happen, my parents are able to quickly assess the situation and move things toward a positive outcome. They rarely get paralyzed and I think this is generally because they have a strong faith in God and that things happen for a reason and will usually work out. We saw this kind of thing play out numerous times on our trip around the world when something completely unexpected or unplanned happened.

In the meantime, Papa and Grandma had shown up and Mom, Isabelle, Trinity, and I piled into my grandparents' car.

"Scoot over, Trinity," I said.

"I am over," she said.

The car was a bit small for the four of us plus both grandparents, but we were on a mission to make the flight. Trinity was pretty angry about the situation and blurted out, "This isn't fair! This is a crisis!" Just then we drove past a homeless tent village under the highway and Mom said, "No, Trinity, that is a crisis."

By the time we caught up with Dad, he had found the car and paid to have it released from impound and we piled in the rental car, said goodbye again to our grandparents, and raced to the rental car return. I didn't want to miss any more school than was necessary either and so we darted through the terminal in a dress and heels with my family

Put in the work ahead of time to ensure full preparation.

trailing close behind. Now, if there was an award for miles run through airports, we would probably win it. It's incredible the number of times we've had to run through an airport and literally been the last people on the plane with the door closing directly behind us. Because of how frequently this has happened over the last 10 years, we know not to check bags because that slows down the whole process.

Already out of breath at security, I tossed my heels into the tray to be scanned and continuously peeked at my watch. Just as I neared the gate, the attendant announced the final boarding call. I zipped down the jet bridge behind the other passengers and collapsed into my seat.

So…another takeaway? Pay the right parking attendant.

• • •

The Galleria Installation

Isabelle

4,000 paper butterflies. Yes, you read that number correctly. While I have a reputation for pushing the limits, dreaming big, and wanting to expand parameters, even I was surprised as I prepped for our largest installation to date at the Galleria mall, **From Fold to Flight**, in Dallas that May. This first large-scale operation included 4,000 large origami butterflies.

I'm grateful for our connection with the Crow Museum and when they were asked about an origami installation for the Galleria Dallas mall they suggested calling us. I love that and we were eager to hear what they had in mind. After school one day we drove to the mall to meet with Martha Hinojosa, who led the mall's public relations department at the time. She is such a fun, creative person and we loved working with her right from the start. After two hours of brainstorming ideas and talking about logistics in the boardroom, Martha asked, "Do you want to see the space?" We walked down the mall and up to a railing above the ice rink. Standing on the third-floor balcony I scanned the *huge* open four-story space.

Looking at the space, all I saw were flickers of opportunity. *This is going to be so awesome. If we manage to pull this off, this is going to be the most epic thing we've ever done!* I couldn't wait to get started and I had no idea that Katherine and Mom were thinking something completely different. Katherine and Mom didn't think it was humanly possible.

"Is this physically possible? Is this something we could actually do?" was running through Katherine's head.

Days later, Mom told me that in her head she was thinking, *No, we just need to say no right now. Thank you for the offer, but we don't want to waste any more of your time. Yep, we need to say no right now and walk away to our car, and go home. How in the world would we ever have the time to complete a project that could fill this space?*

The reason Mom didn't say anything was that I was so happy and excited she just couldn't bring herself to say the words. We left for the car and my mind was spinning with ideas and possibilities.

Thankfully the next morning at my mom's Bible study the lecture leader said to the group of hundreds of women in the sanctuary that "if you never get out of your comfort zone, then you never need God to show up." That immediately silenced the negative chatter in my mom's head and she knew she needed to get on board with my plan.

Our next meeting lasted for hours as we hashed out the details and created solutions to the challenges ahead. We'd taken several samples of paper and sizes of butterflies to the meeting. *How big can we go without an internal frame? How will we hang everything? How many butterflies will we need? What would be the easiest design for volunteers to make? How long would it take? How in the world do we hang this from the catwalk by the ceiling?*

It was a bit crazy, the four-story space was roughly 65 feet across. After the meeting, it came down to logistics and supplies as we considered how much metal framing and wire we were going to need to construct the thousands of suspended butterflies. Another day after school we met with Don and Meredith Clampitt to see about paper sourcing and asked them for a referral of anyone who did large-scale installations. They happened to be meeting the next day with someone who did just that. Mr. Clampitt connected us with the installation company, and we started working with them on the design pattern and installation logistics. We love Don and Meredith and Scott and the whole team at Clampitt Paper. They have helped us make countless projects possible over the years. We had a plan and now we just needed 4,000 butterflies.

Over the next few months, we worked relentlessly on the actual making of the butterflies. At every single folding party held, we only made butterflies. Fossil organized a volunteer day at their headquarters and we made lots of butterflies. Our Tuesday volunteer group, The Paper Dolls, focused just on butterflies. It seemed like people came over to our house almost every day to help make butterflies. Tons and tons of people came over to fold and even took paper home to help us create them. At church, several of the Sunday school classes folded butterflies. In the end, hundreds of people had helped us fold the 4,000 butterflies. At one point, every one of those 4,000 butterflies was in our home, leaving only a narrow path in the hallway. After they were folded, we had to individually attach a hook to every single one. I remember volunteers standing at our counter, looking a bit robotic, stapling butterfly after butterfly. Four thousand may not seem like a big number but when you do the math: 5 minutes to fold, 1 minute to staple each twice and attach a hook, 6 minutes total a piece x 4,000 = 24,000 minutes, or 400 hours, or 1 person working full time 40 hours per work for 10 weeks! Crazy, isn't it?!?

The day before the installation, volunteers came for hours to help begin laying out the drop lines and clipping on the butterflies in a huge empty retail space in the mall. We ran out of space and would need to finish the rest the next night of the installation. We began prepping at 6 p.m. on a Sunday night when the mall closed and had been told that we had to finish by 2 a.m. or we'd need to come back the next night at 10 p.m. to finish. Thankfully tons of volunteers showed up to help.

We were very organized and my mom had posted the patterns and diagrams around the ice rink space where we worked. All around the rink volunteers spaced out the twenty- and thirty-foot wires to individually label them with numbers and letters while others followed to place the butterflies in the correct spots. Another group of people clipped the butterflies onto the wires with carabiners before the next group carried them from the workspace out onto the ice-skating rink. Most of the rink was covered with cardboard to protect the ice and our volunteers.

I raced against the clock and despite having standardized testing the next day, I stayed until nearly 11 p.m. Most of the younger volunteers had to leave to get home because of school the next day, but thankfully dozens of older volunteers stayed till the end and they finished up just before 2 a.m. I viewed this installation as my baby, and I loved to see the fruits of the labor, but it took a while to truly sink in. After a day or two had passed, we revisited the mall and when I looked at it in the light with all the people in the mall, I thought, *This is a thing now. I can't believe we did this.* It really blew my mind that we were able to do something that huge.

Our Biggest Challenge Yet

The butterfly installation was only supposed to be up for two months, but the Galleria extended it through the summer, which gave us more opportunities to utilize the space and installation. At a monthly folding event there, we blocked off a portion of a wide hallway and set up tables and chairs where anyone could stop by and fold. Some people would come up and say, "That's the coolest installation; I want to learn how to do that." It really opened us up to a whole new audience to educate about the water crisis and origami as an art form. A week after the installation we had a big event for the public with tall signage totems with information on everything from the world water crisis, the history of origami, our volunteers and mission, and of course our sponsors. Ekaterina flew all the way from California to do live folding demonstrations and hundreds of people turned out for the event.

I remember one Saturday in particular during the summer installation. We had arrived for a folding event and saw that there were two or three large parties of girls and their dates. In each of the parties of young people, there was one girl celebrating her quinceañera. (For those of you who don't have a large Hispanic population in your community, this is the biggest blowout, an amazing party for girls turning 15.) In one of the parties, there was this gorgeous girl with an amazing red dress embroidered with golden butterflies. She had a golden butterfly necklace on to boot! I rushed over to her and got her to sign a photo release and then rushed to find my dad with his camera and we took several pictures of her with the installation behind her. It was like watching the sunset over a beautiful mountain. It was perfect!

I wish the installation could've stayed forever, so I was sad to see it come down. We'd been recruiting volunteers and had maybe a dozen, but luckily, a newspaper article published that morning invited people to help. What a blessing to have new people we'd never met show up to help. We had about sixty people helping. It happened to be the night before the first day of school and I can't tell you how grateful I was for so much help. We actually completely finished the take-down by 10 p.m. All in we calculated that this project had required 1,000 volunteer hours from start to finish.

The butterflies flew on to all kinds of spaces and places. They got a second life at a Scottish Rite fundraiser, our pediatrician's office, the cafeteria of a summer camp for kids with Down's Syndrome, church and school classroom decorations, and even a future fundraiser for Paper for Water in the backyard of some friends. We learned a lot and the experience built our confidence for doing future installations, although that remains the largest we've ever completed.

Over the time the origami installation hung at the Galleria, there was a twofold increase in foot traffic and a massive threefold surge in social media participation. The installation garnered amazing publicity and shared our mission with thousands of people. Not bad for winging the entire thing.

• • •

The Crow Installation

Isabelle

The installation we did was a permanent ceiling installation at the Crow Museum of Asian Art in the newly renovated gift shop space. Everything we'd done prior for the Crow had been temporary, so for this special one, we collaborated with our dear friend, Russian origami artist, Ekaterina Lukasheva. We needed a wow design to celebrate the opening of their new gift shop space.

The whole thing was a rush job. I think we had a month to pull it all together and were frantically emailing back and forth, *What kind of paper do you want? What shapes?* At one point, I realized that we were in a serious time crunch and decided that we were going to have to pick something, go with it, and hope they liked it.

So Mom and I decided to cover a section of the Crow's ceiling in origami tessellations, which are basically repeating patterns of paper. The tricky part is that you're making a curved fold on a flat piece of paper and every piece of paper needs to be pre-scored. Otherwise, you can't fold it. We had gone to Clampitt for the paper and mailed a lot of it to Ekaterina, who used her special machine for scoring paper and mailed them back to us in giant boxes. She had also completed a ton of the pieces, so that saved a huge amount of time.

After the boxes of tessellations arrived, Mom and I racked our brains for how in the world we were going to hang them. I'm not sure why I chose to get creative with this project, but I knew I wanted to hang them flat rather than on edge. Typically, we hang things on an edge and it's easy because you just poke a hole and set up a loop through it. To hang them flat, we needed to find a way to attach the strings to make sure they weren't going to tilt. They needed to be completely level. Since the tessellations are essentially flat, there wasn't an easy way to do that.

Our solution was the most complex hanging system we've ever done to date and was totally overengineered. I'm sure we could have done something simpler, but we ended up using three to four pieces of fishing line per tessellation and started gluing them on the circle equally spaced apart. I spaced the fishing line attachments at three points equidistant from each other. I realized the glue wasn't working, so I had to grab some special tape and then pray that the tape didn't pull off.

I did the vast majority of the tessellation hangers by myself, which was horrible. For each one, I put glue on the string, put the tape on top of the glue, and then added more glue when the old glue dried. Once everything was fully dried, the flat tessellation would have three little pieces of fishing wire sticking straight up. I'd then gather them all together and put a crimp bead on the slightly longer string to be able to actually hang it.

The Crow had set up a straight wire structure seemingly hanging in the space. So on the day of the install, my mom and I took the strings and connected them by attaching a loop and a fishing hook. Yep, that's right, a barrel swivel fishing hook. We've used all kinds of things to make our installations work. We'd stood on ladders for hours to install the tessellations, and when I hopped down to view our work, my stomach dropped. *They look terrible.* There were too many and a lot of them were the wrong length.

Mom and I had used our design pattern and had gone over the exact placement of every single one and thought they'd look great in the space.

"Mom," I said, "We need to completely rethink the pieces and the placement."

A bit defeated, I trudged along. We ended up removing a lot of the tessellations to help with the overcrowding and went in to individually adjust all the lengths. The result was awesome, but it was a painful process and took so much work to get to that place. Thankfully the fishing hooks helped make it easy to remove and rehang each piece. We ended up working the next day after school until 10 p.m. the night before the reopening, to get the look just right.

It was so fun to be part of the party the next night and I felt proud to have contributed something that would last for years to come. I was grateful to the museum for the opportunity and to Ekaterina for helping to make it all possible.

• • •

Well Done 2020

Travis Nolan is an amazing person! He is an amateur paleontologist, a straight-A student, a master origami artist, and because God, as always, knows what Paper For Water needs, Travis started volunteering with PFW in 2018. After volunteering with us for a pretty short period of time, he came to us with a plan that he and his parents had cooked up and we loved it! Travis was a junior at Cistercian Preparatory School (an all-boys school that Dad happened to graduate from way back when). The juniors have a ceremony in the fall of their junior year where they receive their senior rings. The juniors also plan a big classwide project that they hope will have a long-term impact. Travis decided that he was going to convince his classmates that they should do a major water project at a boys' school in Kenya and fundraise for it themselves. With his infectious enthusiasm and organizational skills, he put a proposal together that his classmates agreed to and they announced their plan at their Senior Ring Ceremony.

Travis then proceeded to take every speaking opportunity we had that had a speaker's honorarium and even some that didn't. He and his classmates helped at gift fairs and folding events to create and market origami ornaments. Travis was a powerhouse and led his classmates on this year-long project that they appropriately named Well Done 2020 (the year they would all graduate high school.) Travis and his classmates raised $20,000 to fund a water tower, a water tank, a well, and a submersible pump and storage building that was installed at the St. Michael's Muluwa Secondary Boys' School in Kakamega, Kenya. There were 1,036 students, teachers, and administrative staff at the school who previously had to walk four kilometers round trip to bring water to their classrooms from a spring that was from a contaminated groundwater source. Since the installation of the complex water system, class attendance has increased because the boys are healthier and each night the boys are able to take clean water home to their families.

After the project was completed, Travis continued to volunteer with us. In a few pages, Katherine writes about the advent of the Change Makers' Council but when I think back to Travis' work on the Well Done 2020 project I think that is where I realized that we needed more youth like Travis.

2019
CONSCIOUS LEADERSHIP

> *"We always overestimate the change that will occur*
> *in the next two years and underestimate the change*
> *that will occur in the next ten."*
> Bill Gates

EarthX Texas

Isabelle

Over the years, two components that have helped us thrive have been our willingness to learn as we grow and to obtain inspiration from others. Having visited the locations of several water projects, we'd experienced firsthand the change we'd been able to make as two young women, yet our growth posed a question for us as well. *How might we continue to scale our educational efforts, teach our philanthropic values, and inspire the change in more youth?* We'd never backed down from a challenge, and 2019 would prove no different.

Despite being a crazy day, I look forward to EarthX Texas every year because there is magic amidst the mania. Early that spring proved no different as excited chatter filled Centennial Hall. Now, at EarthX, you have to pay to have a booth. Normally, we do not go to events that require us to pay, and gratefully, Clampitt Paper sponsored our booth. This was very helpful because otherwise, we wouldn't have gone at all. Early in the morning, I arrived with Katherine and my mom. A bunch of volunteers had signed up to run the booth and talk to people, teach them how to fold origami, tell people about the water crisis, and all that fun stuff. I had maybe five minutes at our booth because Katherine and I were so busy doing other things.

Right at the beginning of the event, one of the organizers came up and said, "You need to go do this interview right now. She's super into environmental journalism."

I knew we were doing an interview with speaker and author Mark Victor Hansen, *who co-created the iconic series Chicken Soup for the Soul*, at some point that day, but I don't think we'd planned on that interview. We'd barely finished it when we had to dash to the next at another building, which is where we met one of the Sea Shepherd guys.

Sea Shepherd is an incredible ocean conservation organization that acts almost like modern-day, reverse pirates who attack whaling vessels and force them to stop. Hearing the tail end of one of their stories, I was in awe of their level of dedication. Seeing other people fully committed and hearing how willing they are to do whatever it takes to accomplish their projects always adds strength to our mission. The conviction behind what they do is inspiring and moving.

One of the cool things about our interview with Mark Victor Hansen was all the awesome people in the audience. We actually ended up meeting the CEO of Lion's Gate. We've almost had a documentary so many times over the years or we've almost been a part of a documentary, but nothing has ever been finished and released. I don't know if anything ever came of the meeting (yet). But who knows what could happen with that in the future?

And speaking of films, on the day after one of our interviews, I was about to walk out of the building when I noticed a sign on the wall for a movie that was about to play. *Ya mean there are movies here too? That one looks cool.*

"We should go watch that," I said.

I hadn't known that EarthX was a pretty major film festival for environmental movies too. One of the movies featured a project by Jacques Cousteau's granddaughter that helps save indigenous people in Brazil. Coincidentally, I'd had the opportunity to speak with her for a couple of minutes while taking promotional photos. Not only was it cool to meet that incredible family, but it was also neat to chat with her about her work and to see how her project related to some of the things we do, especially for our projects in the Amazon rainforest.

Seeing other people fully committed and hearing how willing they are to do whatever it takes to accomplish their projects always adds strength to our mission.

It's important to help those indigenous communities get the resources they need so that they don't die out. They are essentially the protectors of the rainforest, and they're the only thing stopping companies from being able to come in and clear-cut everything. It's very near and dear to our hearts.

Mom and I ended up staying at the event longer to watch the Sea Shepherds' movie. I definitely plan on going to more of the film festivals in the future, and who knows, maybe one day I will be there to showcase our documentary.

• • •

Returning to the Reservation

Katherine

In June, I returned to the Navajo Nation reservation for a week-long trip. Isabelle had gone with five of her friends to volunteer the year before, and since they'd all enjoyed the experience, I wanted to take some of my friends there too. Over the years, I've become close with many in the Navajo community of Smith Lake. Ever since my first trip to Smith Lake four years prior, I could see how they might feel forgotten, and after putting myself in their shoes, I wanted them to feel seen and heard.

> *A lot of people go out there to try and fix the issue. They think it's going to be solved quickly, and they're going to go home feeling good. Then when they encounter a difficult issue to work through, they do as much as they can and never go back. Several people on several different occasions even said, "Oh, you've come back." So, I think the recurring trips have really fostered a good relationship between the people, the organization DigDeep, and us. We kept going back, and we've now been doing it for five or six years.*

After the long drive there, my friends and I all piled into a hotel. Typically, our **Paper for Water** groups stay together in a mobile home on the reservation, but there was another group volunteering this time who were staying in our usual place. Each day there, we woke up and set out on different tasks.

One day, Darlene took us around in the water truck for the tank deliveries. Usually, while visiting the people, we'd give out school supplies and blankets. That year, we also partnered with a church group from Mississippi that puts together buckets and bags of food and supplies. So we spent one or two days packing the buckets and then helped bring those around. I could see the shock pass over my friends' faces.

One of my friends commented after seeing the living conditions, "Wow, just wow. I mean I knew poverty existed in Central and South

America. And everyone thinks about Africa and India, and all those countries and continents being impoverished and in need, but no one thinks about New Mexico. Nobody thinks about the United States. Nobody thinks about the people right here in our backyard."

She was in shock, and her comment reminded me of my first visit to Smith Lake. It's kind of similar to the whole world water crisis, which many people don't even know about. It is the exact same thing with people here in the United States without water—people just don't know.

It's a great experience for any young person to have, both volunteering and immersion into another culture. It's not something you get to experience on a daily basis. I think for the majority of my friends, it also expanded their awareness. Several of them have been to developing countries, but the majority of them had not. Sure, you see poverty

It's a great experience for any young person to have, both volunteering and immersion into another culture.

here in Dallas and some other places, but nothing too extreme, nothing really glaring. Just to be able to drive to the next state over and see people without running water, without electricity, without plumbing, without the bare basics is really eye-opening.

The return trips to the reservation and getting to see everyone who had water and then also seeing still so many with a huge need motivated us to keep going. For every home we'd go to with water, we drove by another one without. Yet every year the range of people with water and the areas of people with water in their houses progressively grows.

However, after coming back from that trip, sometimes it feels like things were moving too slowly and that nothing has really happened.

It seemed like the project was taking forever. For a while after the Kleenex video, we were super amped up about the project. The video helped generate traction and raise a lot of money. After riding the high of that, I fell into a bit of a slump and thought the project was taking too long. At some point, we raised money for a backhoe for DigDeep because theirs had broken. They weren't able to dig more projects or do anything for a while before they received it. It was setback after setback, and it felt like it wasn't going anywhere. But through it all, we stuck it out and I'm so glad we did.

By Christmas of that same year, we finally helped complete the last home in the Smith Lake Navajo reservation area. We'd been working with them on the project for about four years at that point. It was incredibly rewarding to see it completed and had a friend come to our house to film a YouTube video to thank everyone for their support over the years on this project.

I will be up-front: I kind of hate filming YouTube videos. We usually try to do more than one at a time. It's just a long period of time spent forgetting lines and messing up words. I hate having to try and fake emotions or be overly happy, but this video was easy to film. There was no need for faking or retakes. We all just talked about the difference made for all the families who lived on the Navajo reservation. I felt so proud getting to make that video. Sometimes I feel like I can't be proud of everything I've accomplished because without my family, volunteers, and donors I wouldn't be able to have the impact I have and accomplish the things I do. I also never want to come off as all full of myself, but this project made me feel really proud. It was a huge, long-term project and I'd stuck with it, from start to finish, even when it was hard.

With our other well-drilling projects, Living Water is the entity, the boots on the ground, who are then with the community for the years after. They are the ones who get to see firsthand the growth and the ripple effects the project has for the people. After we receive the well report, it's kind of like we're done with the community

> *because we aren't the entity that implemented the actual well. However, with the Navajo Nation, we felt deeply connected to the work we were doing there. We could see the fruit of the labor over four years. We got to see all of these families and all of these houses that now had a sink, a shower, and electricity. It was an incredibly rewarding experience that I think is also a great example of persevering because it was really difficult.*

. . .

Ernst & Young Entrepreneur of the Year Award

Katherine

Juggling school, sports, and **Paper for Water** can be tough at times. Thankfully, we have our board members and parents to help us out with different tasks, like researching and applying for various awards. In 2019, our dad submitted an online application to nominate us for the Ernst & Young Entrepreneurs of the Year Award. The Ernst & Young entrepreneur program is dedicated to recognizing "unbounded ambitions delivering innovation, growth, and prosperity that transform our world."

Apparently, Ernst & Young couldn't give that specific award to us because we are a nonprofit organization. However, the committee reviewing applications liked our project so much that they created another category within their event so that we could actually receive an award from them, or I guess I should say, one person in particular. Turns out, the person leading the evaluation of all the applications for the award was actually the father of one of my former classmates and I'd folded with his daughter at a small event.

From the beginning, I've been a little weird with intermingling friends from school with **Paper for Water** and events. Although, there is definitely something to be said about the value of connections made, regardless of how they originated. I've done a couple of events with my former classmates, like a hot chocolate and folding party. That type of event kind of falls into the category of being not one that I particularly like, not one **Paper for Water** is getting paid for, and not one I see directly adding a superb benefit to the organization—which can also be known as being between a rock in a hard place when it comes to communicating that.

When I think about what the best use of my time is, I don't jump to that type of event. When I don't see a super clear benefit, I'm a bit iffy, but this is one of the great examples of doing events that I'm not instantly down to do. I don't know if he would've been as apt to create another category for us had his daughter not been involved with us before. This is a great example to make as many connections as you can with people. Even if you're going to the event just to make and foster connections, it's still a good use of time.

Make as many connections as you can with people.

The actual Ernst & Young award ceremony was super fun. Remember my mom's homestay sister, Megumi? Her daughter, Mocha, had come to stay with us for two months and had the opportunity to go too. And of course, our grandma and papa came to cheer us on too. After we arrived at the gala with over 2,500 attendees, Mocha looked around in awe and asked, "Is this what you guys get to go to all the time?"

Laughing, I quickly told her, "No, no, this is literally once in a lifetime for us. This is definitely not the norm."

Trust me, it's not always this glamorous. After devouring some of the best hors d'oeuvres I've ever had in my life, my attention shifted to the moment Trinity, Isabelle, and I would accept the award. Now,

I've had trouble keeping my balance in hiking boots, let alone high heels! Thankfully, we didn't have to prepare a speech, so I didn't have any nervous jitters about speaking to the large crowd. Instead, the nerves were all directed towards not tripping in my very unstable and uncomfortable heels. I'm pretty sure I wobbled all the way up the steps, thinking, *Don't trip, don't trip, don't trip.*

Before this Ernst & Young award, I don't think we'd ever had a category created for us. And while this allowed us to be recognized on the regional level, we were unable to go on to the national level. I now know the application process and who knows where the connections made at the event will lead. I feel like we made it to the event because we had fostered connections, and now I think the result of fostering connections at the event and making new connections there will in turn help us down the line. Isabelle and I have found that so many things are about who you know and what connections you have. For instance, when you know someone within a company, you can get in a whole lot easier than approaching them like everyone else.

If I ever start my own business or go into the world of business in any capacity, I have incredible connections in business, culinary, retail, just to name a few. I've amassed an insane pool of connections over the last ten years, which will potentially be very helpful in the future, depending on what I do with my life. I guess that's the only part I still need to figure out. ;)

• • •

The Change Makers' Council

Katherine

"Let's see which one of these meetings could have been an email…"

"People who enjoy meetings should not be in charge of anything." –Thomas Sowell

"If you had to identify, in one word, the reason why the human race has not achieved, and never will achieve, its full potential, that word would be 'meetings'" –Dave Barry

"Committee—a group of men who individually can do nothing but as a group decide that nothing can be done." –Fred Allen

"If you want to build a ship, don't drum up the people to gather wood, divide the work, and give orders. Instead, teach them to yearn for the vast and endless sea." –Antoine de Saint-Exupéry

Little kids inherently know that meetings are boring. Usually, it's because kids don't understand what is being discussed or they aren't being brought into the discussion to think that their opinion matters. My dad once commented that the first time he was in a boardroom with real decision-makers and making real decisions, he was in his early thirties. He told me that it was a steep learning curve from the basics of *Robert's Rules of Order* to agendas and how to run effective meetings that actually accomplish something. At fifty years old, he says that even working in a Fortune 10 company, he still routinely shows up to ineffectively run meetings. Early on, he sat Isabelle and me down and said, "I want you to learn how to run an effective meeting."

I don't remember my first **Paper for Water** board meeting, but I couldn't have been more than seven years old. What I do remember about those early board meetings is that I often spent the majority of the meeting drawing pictures. When I was a little toddler, I didn't start actually talking until I was three or four. I didn't need to; Isabelle did all the talking for me and almost always expressed my needs. I never wanted for anything. There was a brief point in our public-speaking career when Isabelle suddenly became shy. I had about a year to take the spotlight and shine, but that shyness evaporated pretty quickly, and Isabelle's desire to lead returned. So in those early meetings, Isabelle did most of the talking.

Somewhere around 2014 or 2015, I started participating more. I knew the material being discussed like the back of my hand. I mean, I did lecture to adults on pretty much a weekly basis. And having been in so many board meetings soaking up the discussions around me, I felt much more comfortable making my voice heard.

Now that I'm fifteen, I have no problem making sure that when I have a differing opinion that needs to be expressed, the group hears it. More recently, in November of 2020, I won The Indianapolis Children's Museum Power of Children Award and was given a similar opportunity to teach others in a symposium. The symposium offered beginner to advanced classes and featured topics such as raising money, cultivating donors, and transitioning to the online fundraising space. I was to lead a class on crafting an elevator speech and the importance of communicating your message, and I was in a planning meeting with a large group of college-age young adults that were responsible for running the conference where I'd been asked to speak.

The young lady introducing me and leading my section appeared to have never done this before. Putting the presentation together, it became painfully obvious to me that we were going to lose our teen audience before we even started. She'd crafted a PowerPoint Presentation using the Curlz MT font and had way too many unicorns and rainbows. There wasn't much real content in her PowerPoint, and we were supposed to be explaining to these teens the fundamentals of nonprofit fund-raising.

I politely explained that these were teenagers, not young children and that I could use one of my old presentations on fundraising and create material that would fill the 45 minutes and treat these teenagers like mature youth.

These types of interactions have made us realize in 2019 that over the last eight years, we'd been given an amazing gift. We wanted to share that gift with other teens our age and younger. As a board, we'd been batting around the idea of having a youth board for quite some time. There was a little pushback from our legal representatives on the board about actually calling the youth board a real board because of any issues that might arise with our charter. So we decided to call it a council, The Change Makers Council.

Isabelle and I wanted to create real opportunities for youth in our community to plan events and fundraisers from beginning to end, to learn how to run effective meetings and put strategies together for growth, to prepare speeches and deliver them before executives and real-world movers and shakers, and when truly polished in their delivery, to be on TV and tell the world about **Paper for Water.**

We were not only creating our own speaker's bureau, but we were beginning to think about what succession planning will look like when first Isabelle goes to college and then I do.

The Change Makers Council has been a resounding success. Our own board members routinely lead talks that are relevant to starting, growing, and running a business. And just like people are amazed that Isabelle and I can interact with adults and actually have real conversations that don't invoive texting or emojis, our Change Makers have raised thousands of dollars, planned events, and done fantastic interviews on TV! This new chapter expands on our belief that philanthropy and giving back isn't an either/or situation, we believe it can be a both/and situation. You can play sports and be in plays while learning and making a positive impact in the community. You can be a kid and do amazing things!

Our parents believed that we could do more than our age would suggest, and we've found that our peers can do way more than is expected of them by the general populace because we expect great things from them. Over the years, **Paper for Water** has given me an international perspective. There are a lot of late nights and hard days when it seems like the work is endless, but whenever we get to go visit our water projects or have the chance to inspire others, it is worth all the effort. Making a difference doesn't require a massive organization or huge donations. It requires a willingness to start. You may have to start out small, but you're never too young or too old to make a difference in the world.

• • •

Pacific Coast Origami

Isabelle

On the evening of my birthday at the Pacific Coast Origami convention in Oregon, I pondered the creation we'd made in an hour for a giant origami contest. Travis, Katherine, and my cousins had folded a three-headed, four-winged, two-tailed crane out of a square nine-foot piece of paper. Together we'd picked up the edges of the paper and walked them to meet the other side, creasing the paper with our entire bodies and stepping on some of the folds until the dinosaur sprang to life.

"What should we name it?" I asked Travis.

Travis, who was by far the best folder in our group, had directed the challenge and walked around the paper dinosaur.

"Kinda looks like it was born in a nuclear power plant," he said.

We settled on the fantastic title, "Crane-O-Saurus Rex Born in a Nuclear Power Plant," but unfortunately, we didn't win the contest. Hey, our competition was fierce: a fish-man, a giant boat, even a nautilus.

Even though our group didn't claim the prize, the energy of the entire event was contagious and felt like a win in and of itself. People folded around the clock, carrying boxes of paper everywhere they went and attended all-night folding parties in the lobby of the hotel.

While we were there, Katherine and I took several classes with origami masters from around the world. The classes ranged from being super complicated to how to make an easy hat. Our friend Ekatarina, who is a Russian origami genius, taught a class on tessellations that we joined. With the help of a translator, a Japanese master taught an easier class on how to make a fox, and a more challenging class focused on wet folding with heavy paper, where you bend the paper rather than crease it.

I also took a class with my dad centered around using a model, turning the model into a larger piece, and connecting them all. The teacher said, "I've never seen someone combine those in that way before."

I ended up doing it completely wrong, but the final product still turned out cool. I did it so wrong that I did it right. I think, like in life, in the end, it all works out.

When it was time for us to teach a class, we focused less on showing how to make something and more on revitalizing the art of origami in a unique way, introducing others to the art, explaining how we have

I did it so wrong that I did it right. I think, like in life, in the end, it all works out.

taught thousands of people to fold who may have otherwise never learned how. The class gave a unique opportunity to highlight the origami side of our project rather than just the philanthropy, which was neat because rarely is origami the highlight of the presentation.

Everyone was so passionate about origami and excited that younger people wanted to carry on the tradition and teach others. I enjoyed being in a space where everybody loved origami and knew what we were talking about without us having to explain the rudimentary terms.

• • •

EOXCentric

Katherine

Whether in a debate class or on stage in front of thousands of people, I still get nervous when speaking or presenting in front of people.

Everyone always says with time and practice the nerves will subside, but I'm fairly certain that is not true. I know I am capable of public speaking, which is reassuring; however, as far as the nerves go, I think Isabelle is far more comfortable than I am. I do believe that a lot of success is derived from stepping outside of that comfort zone and having my heart attached to a cause that is bigger than myself or my nerves allows me to step onto the stage every time.

In September, Isabelle and I walked onto the stage for the Entrepreneurs' Organization XCentric, a TED Talk-style presentation to C-level executives, at the Omni in downtown Dallas. We didn't know it at the time, but this event would be our last major in-person speaking event before the pandemic.

We were honored to be the only kids attending the event of 550 entrepreneurs. And not only were we the only kids attending, but they'd asked us to speak to all of the adults. The notion alone that we had something that was beneficial for all of these incredibly successful entrepreneurs allowed us to be more confident on stage.

> *Like us, the adults attending the event were seeking to learn something new and to be challenged. Our speech centered on the idea that as entrepreneur to entrepreneur we breathe the same air that anything is possible and drink the same water, that hard work and perseverance win out every time. The idea of a shared value of entrepreneurship, an attitude of always walking around life with our learner's hat on instead of our knower's hat, allows us to see different angles and solve problems in more efficient ways.*

While a lot of the people in attendance may have run companies longer than we'd been alive, we trusted in the accumulated experience and knowledge during our lives and know we also walk common grounds.

> *Having traveled to all seven continents and visited socialist countries, we have become true believers and supporters of capitalism. While* **Paper for Water** *may be a nonprofit, it is built around conscious capitalism. We understand entrepreneurs are the backbone of the economy, and we recognize the importance of crafting innovative solutions to better the world. We are constantly evolving and evaluating business elements such as supply and demand, supply chain management, revenue before expense, social media budget, volunteer management, and leadership training.*

When I saw the schedule, I loved the fact that we opened on the first day because our message had a greater likelihood of reaching more people. We've learned it is challenging to convince adults to take us seriously, so going first made it less likely that the attendees would skip out. That timing proved to be a great opportunity to talk about clean water and convince a group of very successful adults that kids are way more capable than they are often given credit for.

Instead of focusing on fundraising, the speech was geared more toward the lessons we've learned in business and emphasized the organization's unique appeal to people in a variety of settings and age groups. Our speech played on the commonality of their mentorship to younger people in some form or fashion, whether it be their employees, children, nieces, nephews, etc.

We asked them to consider whether they played the short game or the long game within their respective dynamics. A short-game question would be asking whether they have studied for a test on Friday or not, while a long-game mentorship question preps one for greater accomplishments, like college and life-long impact. I've learned a lot about goal setting and my perspective has evolved. I've learned that transformational projects don't occur when we set small goals in short time horizons.

It's hard to explain the impact of long-term involvement, both to others and for oneself. Isabelle and I live in a generation that thinks everything should go viral, and it doesn't. We are reared on social media where approval is instantaneous, and rejection and scorn are permanent. In a reality TV generation, reality is lost because meaningful things take time. Nothing happens overnight. There have been no sudden jumps or massive million-dollar donors. Even when our videos reach more than two million views, Oprah still hasn't called us to be on her show or surprised us with a check.

One could learn so much about life and business by dedicating just four hours every week to a cause.

> *Throughout our journey, our parents and mentors have encouraged us to dream big and have meaningful outcome metrics. Isabelle and I measure our success by the number of leaders we help create, whether that is through Change Makers, by getting kids to think like entrepreneurs, or through opportunities that develop after having been provided clean drinking water. Our success will be measured by how many lives we save and how many girls we can get into school. We aim to be just as impactful as the water and to continue sprouting hope, inspiration, and empowerment.*

• • •

The Wedding Planners

Katherine

Two weeks after the Entrepreneurs' Organization XCentric, **Paper for Water** partnered with the Four Seasons for their annual wedding planner event for a full evening of tasty food and fun. The organizers invited us to come and be a part of this event for wedding planners to help convince them to tell their clients to host their wedding at the Four Seasons. The idea was that if we chatted with the wedding planners, they would tell their clients to have us do the table decorations or centerpieces.

To be honest, neither of us wanted to do the event. School and athletics were picking up and the last thing we wanted to do was drive out to Las Colinas on a school night and stay late folding origami. However, our father convinced us, and we begrudgingly went.

In addition to **Paper for Water**, there were also several other people presenting their ideas to the wedding planners. The event was set up so that the wedding planners were divided into groups and circulated through all the stations. There were some very cool stations, and Isabelle and I were both bummed we couldn't do them with the planners. I really wanted to do the cupcake decorating station, Isabelle wanted to do the flower arranging one, and my dad wanted to do the make your own cocktail station.

With each group, we gave a short presentation about **Paper for Water** and then taught them how to make some simple origami. We also showed off our more elaborate designs in hopes that they would recommend our decorations to their clients. It started out as a rather formal event, but with each new group, we started to have a lot more fun until we got to the groups that had already visited the cocktail station. Then it became absolutely hysterical.

Most people have probably never thought about what it is like to teach intoxicated people how to fold origami to any degree of accuracy. Let me give you an idea: "The first thing you are going to do is fold your paper in half like a rectangle...No that's actually a triangle, let's make a rectangle...The corners actually need to touch or at least be close...Yes, of course, we can help you do it...Here, this is what it is supposed to look like...Yes, you did a great job...All by yourself...no, we're sorry, but your butterfly will not fly for real..."

To say we had a great rest of the evening would be an understatement. We had so much fun teaching these delightful people how to fold. The evening went from being an unpleasant chore to a night of laughter and great food. It's crazy the number of times we have complained about not wanting to go to an event and then had a complete blast.

Isabelle and I left that evening happy that we had gotten to meet so many lovely people and hopeful that we would get a few orders from their clients. And lo and behold, that week we got a huge order.

• • •

Bob Hopkins and Philanthropy Misunderstood

Katherine

One person who has had an influential role on our journey has been Bob Hopkins. When I think about someone who is constantly giving and dedicating themselves to others, I think of Bob. I am so thankful to know him.

Despite being in fundraising and philanthropy for over ten years, I only recently made a rather profound realization. My mom is vital to **Paper for Water.** She is our number-one volunteer and has always helped us keep the organization running smoothly when Isabelle and I have to attend to obligations, like school. However, we are always getting on her case because she has a hard time saying no to people. She is an incredibly generous person and often struggles with turning down opportunities we neither have the time or manpower to do.

As a result, we have ended up attending some events where we didn't raise a lot of money or make many good connections. I have discovered the secret recipe to saying yes and no. As a nonprofit, we work with a lot of big companies because we are able to give them good PR and provide their employees with inspiring volunteer projects. The action is a mutual exchange, both parties benefiting. But with Bob, it has never been an exchange. The difference is that Bob has always had our best interest at heart. Every event and speaking gig we have attended because of him has been because he thought it would help us. Bob has taught us to say yes to potential butterfly flaps. We have learned that his connections and experiences have always been beneficial to us.

Not only did Bob found *Philanthropy* magazine, but he also focuses on teaching philanthropy to kids and college students through his program PAVE (Philanthropy and Volunteerism in Entrepreneurship) and his professorship at Eastfield College.

Bob has fundraised since before we were born with many different organizations and worked to develop philanthropic leaders by teaching about philanthropy and volunteerism. I'm proud to say that we share his vision and hope to inspire the next generation.

Over the years, Bob has taught us a lesson that we still struggle with today. He has imparted to us the importance of saying yes, taking a chance, and showing up no matter what.

Around the time **Paper for Water** started, Isabelle and I enrolled in PAVE. The actual age requirement for the class was ten; I was seven at the time, and I think my parents were really surprised when Bob agreed to let me take the class. The class took an in-depth look at goal setting, brainstorming projects, and mapping out action steps, all things that would later become the foundation of what we teach our Change Makers. While we thought the homework was a little basic, only because we had already been doing a lot of things we were learning, it was fantastic to see so many great lessons compiled into a curriculum for kids. Bob showed us what we already knew: kids are smarter than adults give them credit. The kids in our class embraced the curriculum, digested it, and really engaged in coming up with meaningful projects for what was essentially a capstone project for PAVE graduation. After our graduation, Bob has asked us back many times to talk to his classes, and in 2019, Trinity graduated from PAVE.

Bob has opened up a lot of doors for us since we first took his class. We have attended a lot, *a lot*, of events with him. Every time he calls or emails us about an opportunity, we say yes. We say yes despite not always being incredibly thrilled about going. Don't get me wrong, I love going to a lot of events, but sometimes I just get tired. We say yes because we know how many seemingly unimportant connections we have made at events like these that later down the line have had a profound impact on our ministry. I am not saying you should say yes to everything. You need to know your limits and value your time, spending it in ways that will have the greatest impact and further your goals. Over the years we (and by we, I mean mostly my mom) have gotten better at saying no. But we always say yes to Bob because he has always said yes to us.

So in October of 2019, when we were asked to attend his events for the release of his book *Philanthropy Misunderstood*, I thought it'd be a great place to spread our message and interact with others of similar mindsets. *Philanthropy Misunderstood* featured 108 stories of people who have helped change the world, and we are honored to be a part of the book.

The book events were like a meet-up story swap, and attending them

You need to know your limits and value your time, spending it in ways that will have the greatest impact and further your goals.

brought the inspiration and people from the pages to life. The book is full of stories of people like us who have done some sort of project or helped change lives somewhere in the world. We not only got to tell a lot of new people about our story, but we got to hear other amazing stories.

I think one finds inspiration and hope as often as they look for it, but I also hope to provide ample resources for others to find, whether it's through this book or another avenue. More recently, I actually had the opportunity to connect someone else to Bob. One of my fellow Power of Children awardees was working in Bangladesh and reached out about being in a lull during Covid. She was having difficulty shifting to being online. I gave her some tips and different fundraising models we'd used, but then it occurred to me to introduce her to Bob.

Even though I knew Bob had worked in Bangladesh and had a soft spot for the people there, I didn't really think anything would come of the introduction because sometimes I'll introduce people to each other, and nothing materializes out of it, or they can't really use the connection. But Bob jumped right in there and helped her out. He took time out of his busy schedule to meet with her. And just because of me saying, "Hey Bob, can you just take a look at this real quick?" I hadn't expected that. He truly is a great person and has been wonderful to work with and get to know over the years.

• • •

Texas Country Reporter

Isabelle

Katherine and I grew up without a TV and hadn't seen or heard of the TV program *Texas Country Reporter*. They'd be filming the episode in December during our busiest time of the year and we were pretty tired. Would this be worth it? Do we do it?

"I've never heard of the show, have you?" I asked my mom and Katherine.

While going back and forth about it, Mom chatted with Grandma and received the nudge for us to do it. Our grandma immediately started raving, "Oh, I absolutely love that show. Y'all should definitely do it! Bob and Kelly are famous! I bet tons of people will put in orders for ornaments."

Apparently, **Texas Country Reporter** *is a pretty massive phenomenon, especially in rural Texas. So we agreed to it and invited them to film while we decorated the Four Seasons Christmas tree and hosted a folding session.*

Although they filmed it with us in 2019, the episode wouldn't air until 2020. Honestly, by the time it came out, I'd kinda forgotten about it, but when it aired a little before Thanksgiving, we received over $20K in donations from people we'd never met before. A lot of people gave large donations. The episode is hands down one of our favorites and Bob and Kelly Phillips asked us great questions and helped our mission shine.

That episode of Texas Country Reporter, from the little show we'd never heard of, turned into being the gift that keeps on giving for us because when it aired again in 2021, we received another huge set of orders from the rerun. We will be forever grateful.

Thank goodness we listened to Grandma because she was absolutely right!

Texas Country Reporter

2020
COVID CHRYSALIS

"Water teaches us that we can have great strength to transform even the tallest mountain while being soft, pliable, and flexible."
Assembly of First Nations

Isabelle

A caterpillar grows its wings in isolation, and some could say the world was in its own version of chrysalis during the Covid-19 pandemic. While not trying to undermine the devastation or trauma experienced across the world, for us, 2020 proved to not only be a year of transformation and adaptation but also a year we'd leave with new insights and revelations for the future progression of **Paper for Water.**

Well, this is a bummer. The ski slopes had shut down, and word was circulating about a shutdown just as Katherine and I arrived in Colorado to snowboard for our spring break trip, ready to test out our new boards.

Honestly, when I first heard about the quarantine, I was mostly concerned about school, completing the assignments, and not falling behind. Over the years, I've experienced how schoolwork can stack up quickly from absences. I didn't think of the effect the pandemic would have on the organization because I thought the shutdown would last only a week or two. Then, one week led to the next, then another, and then…another.

I guess what they say is true: "Where this is a will, there is a way" because Katherine and I hiked up on the ski slopes that day. Boarding down the slopes in the crisp air on a bluebird day, I had yet to consider how Covid was going to affect **Paper for Water**. I certainly didn't anticipate the work and adjustments ahead, or that Covid would be like this mountain snowboard experience itself—an uphill climb with no ski lift.

> *Coming into the year off the excitement of 2019, our volunteer recruitment and retention had peaked. We had great donors and were talking with Neiman Marcus about ornaments for Christmas. I fully expected an awesome year on the same trajectory. I assumed the year was going to be even better, and it was to some degree, but certainly not in the ways I'd anticipated.*

Most of our fundraising dollars are generated from in-person events that use the power of volunteers and in-person connections and interactions. So when Korbin and David offered to turn their annual tulip party into a fundraiser, I was thrilled. Now that it was going to be virtual I was a bit apprehensive and skeptical.

Korbin and David are friends and former clients of my mom's and have been supporters of **Paper for Water** for years. Each year, they plant hundreds of tulips and invite friends over for a giant party and lots of delicious homemade food. They had planned to help us before the pandemic, and then they offered to go virtual to keep their commitment to helping a community in Guatemala in need of clean water. After sharing some of our concerns, they stepped up to help and invited us into their backyard for their virtual tulip party. They were way ahead of the curve of what would follow for people worldwide wanting to maintain a sense of connection with others. Honestly, we couldn't have had better hosts—the event was seamless and so much fun. They had spent the whole day decorating their backyard with the last of our Galleria butterflies and making everything look great.

Every half hour, while David made tasty meatballs and pesto pasta, Korbin walked around the garden and showed viewers the beautiful flowers. After the tulip tour, he joined us near our table of ornaments and gave us the opportunity to talk about our mission, the water crisis, and ask for donations. It was exciting to see the donations pour in. We'd drawn a thermometer to indicate the donations on a whiteboard. The donations grew with each segment—as did our surprise. Our confidence for the year increased as the number to raise rose past our $6,000 goal. The event ended up being a huge success, expanding our reach in a new, unexpected way, and ended up providing not just a water project in Guatemala but additional funds toward a bathroom for some school children in Zambia. Thank you, David and Korbin, for persevering for others when it would have been so easy to cancel. You worked so hard to connect new people to our mission and to make the party a huge success.

The party served as an "aha moment" as we learned that we could still raise money without doing something in person. With the success, new seeds were planted, and my overall perception shifted. The fear of not having the one-to-one interaction of years past started to ease, and I began to see how virtual events could be used to reach a larger audience more easily. The virtual event showed the power and effectiveness of virtual platforms and proved to be a great segue and confidence builder for our future fundraising efforts.

• • •

189

Virtual Backgrounds

Isabelle

As the year progressed, it slowly became more and more obvious that Covid was going to last longer than I'd thought. Ultimately, the situation challenged our ability to evolve and spurred innovation. In addition, Kayla was going to be having twins in only two months and we still had our nine-year annual event to plan. We were still hopeful for an in-person event but were learning that the future was pretty unpredictable. We are so incredibly grateful that for a season Becca Reyes came into our lives. She is probably the most talented person that has ever worked for us and could do the equivalent of 40 hours of work in only 15. Even though she landed an amazing full-time position for a large organization, she thankfully still finds time to help us around five hours a week.

We had to come up with new ways to continue raising money, and Covid helped keep us open for input and ideas from others. One person can give you just the right nudge to launch into a creative, new direction. Once again God had brought the right person at the right time.

With our annual event approaching, we tapped into our roots and connected with our community looking to collaborate. Our good friend Shelly Slater owns The Slate, a gorgeous shared office space in the design district. Shelly and her sister created The Slate and it is far more than shared office space. It has a podcast room, collaborative meeting spaces, and a huge recording studio to make every possible event or interview look great. Plus every inch of the building is decorated beautifully and has a feel-good creative vibe. We went really early before school started to record some things for our upcoming virtual annual event. Thankfully Becca had suggested that we take something to hang as a backdrop behind us when recording. Mom remembered that we still had an old installation from a window display at Ivivva at the local mall. That morning we hung those pink and purple butterflies and they looked like they were floating in the air behind us.

Shelly would be recording some things later as our MC for the virtual, so we left up the butterfly display. She loved the butterflies and the way they made the background so interesting. She posted a pic on her social media and pretty soon we had some custom virtual backdrop orders. It felt so good to be so busy and to need help from our volunteers for projects that weren't just creative but that could actually help communities get clean water.

I'd like to take credit here and say that it was my idea to do backdrops, but actually, it was God opening a new door through the help of our friend, Shelly. I love the creative element of designing, visualizing, overseeing production, and building backdrops. I ended up getting

Covid was going to last longer than I'd thought. Ultimately, the situation challenged our ability to evolve and spurred innovation.

up early before school several mornings and working late to finish some of the backdrops on time. But it was very satisfying to have this opportunity to create.

Dallas Baptist University contracted us for a large, 20-foot background project that was probably one of my favorites. This new endeavor showed us that with a little faith, we could thrive amidst adversity. For the rest of the year, **Paper for Water** continued pivoting its strategies and we started to see the silver lining of the Covid cloud. December brought about the start of the most exciting consequence of Covid, the virtual corporate team-building and volunteer events. We started working with companies across the nation and began to see the power of Zoom to bring thousands of people around the globe in contact with our mission.

• • •

9th Annual Event

Katherine

It took months for the pandemic to truly set in for me. I kept thinking, *Two more weeks and I'll be back in school.* Then it was, *By this summer, everything will be back to normal.* But in all honesty, after going hard in 2019, I welcomed the break. The time at home offered a slowdown and gave me a chance to breathe—a nice reprieve from all the go, go, go of the previous years. However, it was difficult not doing so many of the things that make Paper for Water fun.

One of the reasons why there has been so much success with the organization is that Isabelle and I have one another to lean on. I'm so grateful for our working relationship. There's a nice balance that allows us to leverage our strengths and interests while offering support.

It was difficult not doing so many of the things that make Paper for Water fun.

When it was time for our Ninth Annual Event and for me to write the donor letter for our first all-virtual event, I was still a bit surprised that we were this far in the year and still organizing everything online. Holding it virtually had a lot of great positive components. Expenses were lower and people were able to attend who could not have done so otherwise. We even had ten out-of-state event sponsors! The Covid pandemic had made access to water and sanitation more important than ever and donors responded generously. Bathrooms and handwashing stations at schools overseas as well as emergency water tanks for Navajo families had suddenly become our main focus to combat the ever-growing crisis.

Something else had been on the rise with the looming election and that was an increasingly divided and tense atmosphere everywhere we seemed to look. One thing that we love about raising money for water is that it is something that unites us all. After all, whether you are Red or Blue, rich or poor, young or old, American or not, every single person on this planet wakes up with the same basic needs, the most important being access to water. We knew that we needed a speaker to unite our volunteers and donors and we reached out to our friend Adrienne Bankert. We met Adrienne, *ABC News* and *Good Morning America* anchor over a year ago when she interviewed us for a segment on *Good Morning America*. Yes, you read that correctly! We filmed for hours, but sadly in the early morning of our airing, there was a major natural disaster in Indonesia so it was cut way down to just about one minute. It was disappointing, but like Covid interfering with our event plans, there are many things that we can't control. But Adrienne was nice, positive, glamorous, and made a big impression on us. She has a heart for others and a peace about her that really stands out. So it was no surprise that she had just written and released a book on kindness, *Your Hidden Superpower*. That was exactly what we needed for an event happening a week prior to the election and thankfully Adrienne agreed to help us. Her message was inspiring, uniting, and after such a long time of being isolated from friends and family was good for the soul. Adrienne mentioned receiving a letter from me when I was twelve that she had posted on her office bulletin board.

"I do what I do because there are people who aren't able to get on a microphone. So I speak for them."

While a lot of out-of-state volunteers were pleased to attend virtually, the online event did present a challenge. Without our volunteers, we couldn't do what we do. 2020 restricted our in-person recruiting efforts, and we relied heavily on our existing ones. Despite feeling deeper gratitude for our volunteers, it felt harder to emphasize and convey that appreciation through a screen.

We decided to carry over the Youth Volunteer of the Year award and honored ten-year-old William Braskamp, who had been volunteering with us for over two years. William is incredibly intelligent and humble and he is one of our most prolific origami folders. He folds so much that we worry sometimes he is not doing his homework. He has helped with countless projects and we wanted to show our appreciation.

Do you remember the story about setting our ten well, $50,000 goal in August of 2012? The Bible study my mom read that morning was from *One in A Million* written by author and Bible teacher Priscilla Shirer. Priscilla had prayed at our very first event, our five-year anniversary party, and had us speak on her show at her studio in Tennessee. She thankfully agreed to open the event with this beautiful prayer: *"Lord, we are so grateful that you use us for your glory. Thank you, Lord, that these incredible young women and this ministry can be an instrument through which so many people are drawn ultimately to know you. I thank you, Father, for the very practical ways that they are impacting people's lives. I thank you for how they are changing and shifting the trajectory of people's lives in very practical ways. I thank you for all that they've already done, but even now I ask that you would be increasing their territory, would you give them new opportunities, new alliances and relationships, and folks to undergird what it is that you have put in their hearts to do. I pray that you give them even more impact in the days to come than they're even anticipating possible and do what Ephesians 3:20 & 21 says.... Now unto him who is able to do exceedingly, abundantly above and beyond anything that we can ask or think. And Father, we will be careful to give you all of the praise, all the honor, and all the glory. In Jesus' name, amen."*

While doubts for online success had evaporated, I was still surprised that the party turned out to be the most successful event we've ever had. Moving forward, we hope to always include a virtual component to reach more people, but I miss the in-person interactions and look forward to seeing everyone in person in the years to come.

Hearing Adrienne speak at our annual event reinforced the decision to grow the Change Makers' Council during Covid. We've experienced the power of collaboration with all ages and believe the Change Makers Council will be instrumental in our organization's future success.

Despite the challenges, we continued because we know our youth dream big and can accomplish great things, no matter the limitations. Although relatively new, for 2020, we revamped the structure and introduced more of a lesson-style approach for the council's monthly meetings. Some of the lessons included: How to Run an Effective Meeting, Donor Cultivation, Thank You Cards, Marketing & Sending Updates with Newsletters, Crafting an Elevator Speech. This allows our young volunteers to develop leadership and speaking skills, and we benefit from the collaboration and influx of creative ideas and new energy to **Paper for Water.**

"We use art and creativity to help others gain something that is truly life-changing."
– Change Maker council member and volunteer

Nine Year Anniversary Event

Photo by
Meredith Embry

2021
A GRATEFUL HEART

"I've learned that people will forget what you said, people will forget what you did, but people will never forget how you made them feel."
Maya Angelou

Snowmageddon Office Flooding

Isabelle

I guess every flow does have its ebb. Just a few weeks after receiving a Lifetime Achievement Award, **Paper for Water** was hit with another challenge. I think it goes to show us that no matter how many hours we dedicate or how many awards or milestones we achieve, the challenges won't stop.

During Snowmageddon, the pipes froze, and our office flooded. We had no power and found out about the office flooding sometime during the middle of that February week. Our anxiety about the damage kept building because nobody was allowed in the building. The City of Dallas wouldn't let anyone in, not even the people who worked there. The outlets were covered with water, and I guess they didn't want to zap us...any more than our nerves were already doing!

Nobody knew how bad the damage would be. So we just kind of freaked out for a solid week because we had no idea what was happening. When they let us in a week later, they'd said for us to go in and get only personal belongings. My mom said, "We're going to try and get as much stuff out as possible and we will keep working until they make us stop."

I don't blame her. Everything in the office seemed personal to me! A whole team of volunteers came that day, including a church Bible study class that dropped their nets and came as soon as my mom sent the text for help. It was amazing how many people arrived within 30 minutes. Everyone stood on the sopping wet carpet to sort through what was salvageable and what was too damaged to save. A volunteer showed us how the sheetrock would need to be replaced and that we'd need to take everything out of the office. They began boxing up the undamaged ornaments, miscellaneous supplies, everything that could be saved. We tried to salvage as much as possible, but when I look at the photos of the massive piles of trash, I think I was a bit more optimistic going in. For what we salvaged, part of it went to our house, part of it to a friend's garage, and part of it we stored at church.

While we were cleaning the office out, we recorded a couple of videos and compiled those along with a video declaring how we needed help rebuilding. We had been trying to coordinate with The Container Store about organizing our office, but it hadn't worked out until that point. After they watched our video, they reached out and asked, "What can we do? We'd love to help you."

After a couple of calls with them, they set up a design session with their custom closet people. I took some floor plans of our space for a meeting, and with the idea of what we needed, one of their design people walked us through all of our options. They helped us select shelving for storage and volunteer workrooms. One of the silver linings of the flood was that after the sheetrock had been replaced, the walls needed to be repainted in our office. The walls had previously been an unattractive tan color. Katherine would tell you that they weren't that bad, but trust me, every room was a different shade of ugly yellow-brown. Finally, the walls all matched, and they were a bright clean white.

I think overall, it was cool to see how several of our early connections including The Container Store came through for us in one of our most trying times. The relationships we've made over the years never cease to amaze me, and I'm grateful for the continued support. Even though it was a stressful time and a tremendous amount of work to move everything out and then back in, it was wonderful to experience an outpouring of support from both volunteers and donors. It felt like Paper For Water was much bigger than us and way bigger than a huge Texas ice storm and flood. Paper For Water mattered to other people and we are grateful.

• • •

PVSA Lifetime Achievement Award

Isabelle

Honestly, I don't want to make winning this award a huge deal. I think we were the youngest people ever to receive the Lifetime Achievement Award, but there's not a whole lot to say. There wasn't an event. It was a little anticlimactic, which in and of itself is interesting because we'd won a huge award, but it wasn't super special to us. Don't get me wrong, I think it doesn't feel like this monumental thing because it's the accumulation of the past ten years into one number, and it's hard to define all the stories and moments into just one number.

• • •

*Isabelle and Katherine. I'm going to recognize you together despite the fact that you are two distinct individuals who each bring a unique element of service to **Paper for Water**. It's probably unfair that I'm not recognizing you individually, but the two of you together have created what **Paper for Water** is. And that's a youth-run organization that in under ten years has raised over $2.5M and funded over 300 water projects in twenty countries and fundamentally changed the lives of over 85,000 people around the world.*

The two of you together have volunteered an amazing 8,500 hours in the last ten years. To put it in perspective, that is four years of an adult working full time forty hours a week for fifty-two weeks a year with no vacation time. All while excelling at school and sports and having great friendships.

I've been with you two during at least 80 percent of those hours. It's been a LOT of late nights. It's been a LOT of long days. I've missed birthday parties and school events. BUT oh, my gosh, it has been an amazing journey to be on.

The relationships we've made over the years never cease to amaze me, and I'm grateful for the continued support.

We've visited your projects and seen what a transformational impact clean water provides to girls your age in developing countries. We've seen little toddlers running around who we know would have died of parasitic diseases had they been born before the new well was placed in their village. We've seen young girls in school in India getting an education that would have been unavailable to them just one year earlier because they would have been hauling water all day.

A lot of these things I'm recounting are stories you tell on a weekly basis as you educate the world around you about the world water crisis and so they may lose some meaning because you repeat them so much. But I hope that these awards will be framed and hung on a wall in your future offices so that you'll be able to retell these stories and inspire countless people that you meet in the future to see the world through your eyes and convince them as you've convinced all the people in this room that you can make a difference in this world no matter how young or old you are.– Dad

In 2013 we had the opportunity to speak as the kickoff speakers for the Texas Lyceum event on the Southern Methodist University Campus. We spent hours writing and crafting a speech that we subsequently memorized. The speech ended with a call to action and we believe it's worth repeating.

"A lot of people do not even know about the world water crisis. But when we tell them about it, they are anxious to help. Everyone wants to make a difference in the world. God uses all people young and old to make the world a better place. Do something that matters and ask people to help because if everyone helps, it all adds up to a lot.

"A lot of people spend their whole lives waiting. They wait till they are ten so that they are double digits. Then they wait till they are sixteen so that they can drive. Some are waiting until they get a special degree before they start working in their dream job. Others are waiting to make more money or have more free time until then can help other people. Others are waiting too. Waiting for a cup of clean water; waiting for hope; waiting for opportunity; waiting for a pair of shoes; waiting for a coat simply to keep them warm…Do you want to make a difference, change a life, a village, or even our world? Then what are you waiting for?"

WHAT ARE YOU WAITING FOR?

If 5 and 8 year-old girls can decide to go out and change the world, so can you!

EPILOGUE

Since you've read to the end of this book, you don't need me to tell you how incredible the journey these two young women (and their supportive family!) have embarked on is. So instead, I'll attempt to share a glimpse into their impact…into what is perhaps the most ineffable part of our jobs: that moment when someone turns on their tap for the first time.

It would be impossible to describe this experience as a single, monolithic thing. Sometimes the event is met with tears or shouts of happiness. Sometimes you'll see a smile slowly stretch itself across the face of an elderly woman. Other times, hordes of kids—even cousins and neighbors—loudly jostle for position around the sink, waiting to feel the first drops of clean water splash into their outstretched hands.

Perhaps my favorite moments, though, are the quiet ones. Those few, precious times when the client simply opens the faucet, watches the water pour out into the sink, and closes the tap again without saying a word. The simplicity of that moment brings me a different kind of joy—a sense of deep reflection and accomplishment. I get goosebumps just imagining it. Silence is a powerful reminder that while the delight of *finally gaining access to water may explode* out of some people in fits of giggles, access to water itself really doesn't deserve much fanfare. After all, it's our basic human right.

Derrick and Keena Delgarito didn't say a word when they turned on their tap for the first time.

It was a brisk but sunny winter day in 2016 when Katherine and Isabelle joined DigDeep's Navajo Water Project and brought clean, hot-and-cold running water to the Delgaritos' house. We completed that system in secret, while Derrick, Keena, and their four kids were volunteering with a nearby nonprofit. In the late afternoon, just as our shadows started to stretch away from us, Derrick and Keena rounded the drive and stepped out of their car, obviously shocked to see a throng of strangers standing between them and their front door.

After a quick explanation, Derrick walked into the house (one he had built with his own two hands!) and over to his new sink. He lifted his four-year-old daughter up to the tap and helped her wash her hands. When she was finished, he placed her on the floor, turned off the water, and turned around. His face was almost completely blank, but his eyes were a mile deep.

After more than a decade doing this work, these are the moments I remember most. The times that the simple beauty of clean, running water (*right here in my house!*) triggers a quiet wonderment. How I wish it were so for the rest of us, who often take it completely for granted!

I know these are the same moments that power Katherine, Isabelle, and their work at Paper for Water. The giggles and tears and shouts—for sure—but especially those pregnant silences…all folded up together into every piece of origami. What a gift.

George McGraw
Founder & CEO, DigDeep

ACKNOWLEDGMENTS

We would need to double the size of our book to thank every person that has helped and supported us. You might not see your name, but rest assured that your action no matter how small helped us achieve everything that has happened these past ten years. We are grateful for you!

3M—For being our first big grant.

Aitoh Paper—Thank you, Beth, for all the ways you've helped and for a very special day at Micheals we will never forget.

Karla Alfaro—Thank you for all the great advice and your amazing smile and enthusiasm.

Colleen Anderson—You might be our most joyful origami instructor ever! Thank you for all the connections you made for us that led to some big PR opportunities. We hope to see you at Ghost Ranch in the future.

Darlene Arviso—Thank you for showing us that a true hero doesn't wear a cape but works tirelessly for others.

Acknowledgments

Zack Aspegren—Thank you for all your support and for being the best car buddy in Kenya.

Adrienne Bankert—Thank you so much for interviewing us for *Good Morning America* and for being the keynote speaker at our 9th Anniversary Event. You are such an inspiration to us!

Laurence and Rosanne Becker—Your love is so greatly appreciated and your relentless sales work for PFW is legendary.

Eric Bender—Your hospitality, enthusiasm, and postcards are both touching and inspiring.

Mary Bloom—Thank you for hunting us down nearly a decade ago and for making us part of the Crow Collection family. You have always been a great source of inspiration and ideas.

Board Members Past and Present—Your support and insight over the years have been invaluable. Thank you for giving your time and resources to help us grow.

Garrett Boone—Thank you for your inspiration and for supporting us over the years. The Container Store partnership has always been near and dear to our hearts.

BottleRocket—Thank you for all the folding parties and your amazing employees who were probably the best folders we've ever had. And thank you for letting us wear the Storm Trooper gear.

Bruno Brenes—You started our first school club at Jesuit Preparatory School and gave us a glimpse of how we could grow our non-profit. Thank you for helping us learn.

Becky Brown—Thank you for all the lessons and for that day filming with Nickelodeon.

Scott Brown—Thank you for cutting mountains of paper!

Acknowledgments

Leigh, Edwin, and Zoe—Thank you so much for making the office so fantastic, being our official ladder holder, and making great videos with T.

Brodie Bruner—Thank you for all your time dedicated to our board meetings and your, your wife's, and your kids' support of our mission.

Karla Buie—Thank you for being an awesome board member and introducing us to Hedda.

Rugger Burke—Thank you for always providing such wisdom. You've kept us grounded, growing, and inspired.

Change Makers—Your dedication and hard work is inspiring and does not go unnoticed.

Calvin Carter—Thank you for the support during our early years. You were always so fun to talk to with great ideas. We will always remember being on stage with you and your Rocketeers when we presented at your Client Day.

Clampitt Paper—For your beautiful paper and your willingness to cut the hard and large paper. Thank you, Scott and team.

Don and Meredith Clampitt—You always make us smile and feel like we're part of your family. We love hanging out with you and your staff. Thank you for all the EarthX booths and for all your foundation's support over the years.

Sharon Clothier—Thank you for believing in our vision for a PFW exhibit at the Paper Discovery Center and for all the work that went into creating it.

CNN and Jennifer Grubb—Thank you for sharing our mission nationwide.

Scott and Susan Conard—We wouldn't have written this book without your encouragement! Thank you for always being concerned about our mental health and for being one of our longest and most ardent supporters.

Acknowledgments

The Container Store—You always come through with amazing wrapping, effective storage, and killer dance parties.

Julie Cothern—When we needed someone to do our artwork, you stepped up and were so helpful. Thank you for all the work you did to make our graphic artwork spectacular.

Crow Museum—Thank you for all the Family Days, carrying our pieces in your gift shop, the opportunity to decorate your ceiling, and the myriad ways you supported us.

Dallas Morning News—Thank you for being the first newspaper to write about us.

DigDeep—For all the memories. Kleenex, the brown house, the trailer, and the inspiration.

Hedda Dowd—Our professional light switcher and cookie provider. Thank you for everything you do!

Elko Family—The TJ Lemonade stand, all the Stockings and Stuffers, and for all the support over the years, thank you!

The Engstrom Family—We are grateful for all the ways you have helped us over the years.

Shannon Escarra—We miss having you around! India 2013, Neo the Frog.

Carrie Estrella—We had so much fun at Girl Scout Camp and thank you for championing our connection with Kohler.

Exalt Printing—Thank you for all the printing you did for us at cost when we couldn't afford printing fees!

"Uncle" Howard Feldman—Pitching our product to a room full of buyers is terrifying, but you always put us at ease. Thank you for cheering us on to the finish line.

Acknowledgments

Erin Glass and Burke Cherry—For being the most fun producers ever and for helping me with my school musical audition.

Kim Hartner and Howard Feldman—For being the most amazing buyers ever.

Janet Fisher—You have always been our model for how to do Gift Markets. And thank you for creating the Well Wishers. Our partnership with Neiman Marcus wouldn't have been possible without you.

First Reformed Christian Church—thank you for all your support all the way from California.

FUMC Denton—The love we have felt from y'all is amazing. The matching grants of some of your members like Duryea Moving really pushed us to meet our goals.

FUMC Los Alamos—Thank you for your heart for the Navajo and for hosting us at your church. You are such a delightful and generous group of people!

FUMC Orange—You've been supporting us from the beginning. Thank you!

Northaven Methodist—Thank you for letting us preach from the pulpit and telling you all about the world water crisis and for helping fund our cause.

Fossil—We have been blessed by your team so many times. Thank you for everything you have done to help and inspire us.

The Four Seasons Hotel and Resort Las Colinas—We look forward every year to our partnership. Your team is such a delight to work with. Thank you for all the opportunities you have provided us and all the media exposure...and those cookies and hot chocolate are the BEST!

Acknowledgments

Frost Family—We will ALWAYS remember Kenya and Tanzania with you and seeing the white rhinos and mating leopards and the water projects in Kisumu.

Galleria Dallas and Martha Hinojosa—4,000 butterflies! Thank you for the experience of creating something huge and spectacular and being great to work with.

Glenstar Properties—We are forever grateful.

Good Morning America—Thank you for spreading the word about PFW on a national scale.

Good Morning Texas—You were our very first TV experience and we had so much fun.

Greenland Hills Methodist—Your gift market is one of our favorites. Thank you for inviting us to your market every year and for helping us with the Nickelodeon episode.

Edna Guerra—Thank you for taking a chance on us!

Ron Hall—Thank you for being our inspiring keynote speaker at our 5th Anniversary Event and for the podcast and support.

Jackie Harper—Thank you for championing our relationship with The Container Store and for being there for us with donated paper and for helping us after The Freeze.

Michelle Harvey—For believing since the very beginning that this project was worth documenting.

Helen Hiebert—Thank you for fundraising for us and for including Trinity's creations in your calendar and book.

Elizabeth Hildebrand—You and your scrapbook are the reason all of this started.

Acknowledgments

Lyda Hill—You have been one of our biggest supporters. Thank you so much for believing in us and what 2 girls and thousands of volunteers and donors can do to change the world.

Martha Hinojosa—For taking a chance on us even though we had no idea what we were doing.

Amy Hofland—For listening to our dreams and supporting us in so many ways! You gave us so much credibility.

Bob Hopkins—Your love of philanthropy is contagious and we look forward to having you over for waffles sometime soon.

Fred Hoster—For mentoring us.

Stuart Hsu—Thank you for always advocating for us and having us present at your employee forums and for the ability to teach not just your kids but your employees' kids about our love for origami and clean water.

David and Korbin—For your hearts and your commitment and showing us that we could survive Covid.

MaryBeth and Jeff Johnston—Thank you for being one of the first stores to carry our ornaments and for all the encouragement over the years.

Jorge and Rosio—Thank you for keeping us safe in the Peruvian jungle along the Maranon river and for showing us so many of the projects we had helped fund. We can't wait to visit again and how the Village Drill is making a difference.

Karen Katz—For trusting Hedda and believing in us.

Kohler—Thank you for inviting us to meet your team and be part of your gifts that give program.

Elaine Kollaja—For helping PFW become a real official organization and for the DMN article.

Acknowledgments

Kleenex—We loved working with you and hope to do another project with you in the future.

Shelli and Brandon Knutson—Thank you for your generosity and being great event hosts.

Kumar—For showing us India and many of its beautiful places and wonderful people.

Jamie LaBar—Thank you for listening to your parents and reaching out. You hosted our first professional art exhibit and provided us with such great advice.

Ken Lampton—Thank you for your PR at the very beginning. We miss seeing you at Starbucks!

Lemishine—Curtis Eggemeyer—For taking a chance on us at the very beginning and inspiring us to make it more than a one-month project.

Living Water International—Working with you these past 10 years has been an incredible experience. You are such an amazing organization!

Mike Mantel—Your thank-you videos are always the highlight of holidays, can't wait to read your book!

Neiman Marcus—For the once-in-a-lifetime, crazy, awesome opportunity to work with an international brand with so much prestige.

Kayla and Jim McCaffrey—Kayla, we wouldn't be here today if it wasn't for you. Your hard work behind the scenes makes it so much easier for us to do our work. And Jim, you might just be our favorite board member because you found our office space for us. We can't wait for your girls to be the succession plan for PFW.

The McGowan Family—For all those puppies you raised and then donated the proceeds to Paper For Water that brought clean water and the Word to so many. And thank you for our sweet geriatric dog, Sadie.

Acknowledgments

George McGraw—Your love and mentorship has been so meaningful. Thank you for all that you are doing for the Thirsty right here in the USA. You are a real hero!

JD Miller and Lea Fisher—Thank you for hosting our first annual fundraising event.

Holly Hull Miori—You are always our go-to resource on what our non-profit should be doing. Thank you for all your operation insights and your desire to see us grow.

Scott Murray—We still remember when we met you at the AFP event in Irving. Thank you for all the interviews and for being an advocate for so many charities in North Texas.

Nickelodeon—For giving us a chance to reach kids all over the country.

Travis Nolan—Thank you for being such an amazing leader for our youth volunteers and for your incredible dedication.

Nolan Family—For your incredible hearts for others and for raising great kids. Stewart thank you for driving all over the metroplex to take Travis to countless events and the awesome Change Maker campout. Mary, we are grateful for your behind-the-scenes support that helps make it all possible.

NorthPark Presbyterian Church—You've been the backbone of our support for years; we couldn't have done it without you.

Lisa-Adelle and David O'Brien—Thank you for being willing to open your hearts and your home to support our mission. Thank you, David, for your inspiring speeches.

Paper Arts—Terri, Robert, and Miss Pearl. Thank you for always helping us with that difficult-to-find paper.

Acknowledgments

Paper Discovery Center—Paper has been in our family for generations all the way back to Havilah Babcock. Thank you for hosting our installation. Let's do something together again soon!

Paper Dolls—You know who you are and you make so much possible. A special thanks to the team that made Neiman's a reality. You have impacted thousands of lives for the better.

Parkit Market—For every party and gala that you've supported, we thank you! Your generosity is inspiring!

Sister Agatha Yen Pham—Your stunning art inspires our creativity and we are so grateful for your generosity and your prayers.

Pizza Padrone—For all the wonderful pizza and support!

The Porch—Your food is delicious and your generosity is moving. Thank you for making our events great!

Print Team—For your awesome posters and invitations.

Presbyterian Women's Foundation—Your grant was truly a game-changer for the Smith Lake Community.

Providence Christian School of Texas—For support and encouragement from the beginning and for the flexibility to do anything we needed to do.

Frank Ramirez—Thank you for all your help when we didn't know what we were doing as vendors to Neiman Marcus.

Alison Reed—Peru was epic and thanks for letting us crash your wedding.

Becca Reyes—You are probably just about the hardest working person we know. Thank you for all that you do for PFW. We also appreciate how much you are able to calm our mom during stressful times.

Acknowledgments

Erik—Hawaiian Falls. Your amazing heart and your generosity still inspires us.

Risk Theory—Thank you for the opportunity to work with you and your staff. The Christmas employee luncheon in 2019 was fantastic! Your support has been so HUGE to so many of our projects and you have been the foundation of our Christmas Tree Program.

St. Bonaventure—For the opportunity to bring our volunteers to learn from your community and do meaningful work.

Sapio Family—A Billion Entrepreneurs! What an amazing platform to get us to think about how we lift communities out of poverty. Thank you for all your support over the years. You've always inspired us to be bigger and better.

Mike Serinaldi—Our trip out to Michael's is definitely one of the highlights of our early years! You can't imagine how much fun we had and how blessed and surprised we were when we entered your building and all your staff was clapping for us.

Priscilla Shirer—Thank you for your prayers and support and for writing *One in A Million*.

Brian Shultz—From Studio Movie Grill to Look, your growth and success have always inspired us. Thank you for letting us have events at your facilities and for always encouraging us and for giving us great tips on how to bring more people to our cause.

Doug the Bug—The best cameraman out there.

Craig and Anne Sinasac—For keeping PFW going while we were gone and for all the swimming and dinner and for being on our board.

The Slate—Thank you for the beautiful space for our board meetings and for helping us with our videos and most of all for the opportunity to create beautiful backdrops during COVID.

Acknowledgments

Shelly Slater—Best MC ever!

Rand Stagen—Thank you for giving us one of our first major speaking gigs in Dallas and for always encouraging and supporting us.

Mimi Sterling—For helping through the entire Neiman Marcus public relations process and we love your family.

Carrie Stett—Thank you for bringing our passion to help US families to life.

Stringfield Family—Thank you, Abby and Maddison, for your tenacious commitment, and thank you Mr. and Mrs. Stringfield, for supporting us from the beginning.

Talulah & HESS—We love your store and your tremendous support. We are honored to be featured each Christmas.

Texas Health Resources—Thank you for ReVive 2015 and for hosting our Nickelodeon Premiere. Thank you, Mr. Doug Hawthorne, Dr. Britt Barrett, Mr. Jim Berg, and Mr. Jim Parobek.

Mary Sean Thornhill—For all the love, even before Paper for Water started.

Vail Tolbert—We are so fortunate we met you through the Four Seasons. Thank you for all that you've brought to our team. We love working with you.

Vardeman Family—thank you for chairing our 8th anniversary event and for being so amazingly supportive of our efforts since Chicago.

Carlos and Lynne Vaz—Our partnership with CONTI has given our Change Makers such great opportunities. Presenting at your events has been an amazing opportunity to have our Change Makers deliver their highly rehearsed presentations. Thank you for all your support and for your desire for all to have water and the Word!

Acknowledgments

Jean Wallace—You are definitely in the top 5 of our all-time favorite folders. Your work is always amazing. Thank you so much for the generosity of your time and talents over the years.

Sam and Rosemary Watters—Thank you, Grandma and Papa, for your unconditional support and love and for always coming to every event.

Kay Wayma—Thank you for sharing our mission with your readers.

Weathermatic and Mike Mason—We are so inspired by what your company has done and is doing! What if all companies in America loved the Thirsty the way y'all do?

The Webb Family—thank you for being an inspiration to us. We may never have gone around the world without your example. #NYWC2017—so fun!

Well of the Month Club—Our goal is still to get to one well a month from our recurrent donors. Thank you for supporting us for so many years.

Well Wishers—For all the beautiful flower balls and all the lives you've transformed.

Westminster Presbyterian Church—You've been with us from the beginning, and your workroom is where it all started.

Andy Whisenhunt—For taking a chance on a three- and a five-year old.

Wiemers Family—For the long hours folding paper while playing Settlers.

Wilburn Family—Thank you for supporting the Change Makers and hosting events at your house. Ace and Asher are perfect examples of what we are trying to accomplish with our Change Makers!

Beth Wild—Thank you for all the Aitoh Paper and for brainstorming with us about the future.

Acknowledgments

Wilhelm Family—Luke and Ryan, thanks for being such great friends to Trinity and for coming to our events and supporting Paper For Water with your parents.

Wilspec Technologies—Thank you for coming to our first summer camp at the Four Seasons and for bringing your whole office staff to our 8th annual gala. Your support over the years has been so meaningful to us and Ashley, thank you for being so awesome to our mom. You help keep her sane!

Wisley Family—For being there from the very beginning and your willingness to always show up. Your acting stole the spotlight in the Halo Effect.

In Memory of JJ Baskin—Thank you for getting us in front of the Texas Lyceum.

In Memory of Linda Clark—Thank you for being at one of our first folding parties and for your love of Paper For Water and your love of origami. We miss you!

In Memory of Val Halamandaris—Thank you for your vision of what the world can be if everyone cares for each other.

In Memory of Kelly Robinson—Your Scholastic Reader book helped us reach so many kids across the USA.

In Memory of Wynter Pitts—Your friendship was so meaningful and your writing so powerful. We miss you!

Special Thanks to Tony Jeary, Daniel, Kristin and your whole team!

PAPER F●R WATER

DONATE TO PAPER FOR WATER TODAY

You can help us change the world! Join our goal to fund at least
one well a month by joining our Well of the Month Club
and be one of the 500 world changers donating at least
$10 monthly. With the help of our many volunteers, partners,
and representatives, we have been able to bring clean water
to hundreds of communities around the world.

VISIT paperforwater.org to donate now!